# Strange Forces

# Strange Forces

*by*
Leopoldo Lugones

*translated with a foreword by*
Gilbert Alter-Gilbert

Latin American Literary Review Press
Series: Discoveries
2001

The Latin American Literary Review Press publishes Latin American
creative writing under the series title Discoveries
and critical works under the series title Explorations.

Library of Congress Cataloging-in -Publication Data:


Lugones, Leopoldo, 1874-1938.
    [Fuerzas extrañas. English]
    Strange Forces / by Leopoldo Lugones ; translated from the Spanish
    by Gilbert Alter-Gilbert.
            p. cm.--(Series Discoveries)
        ISBN 1-891270-0502 (alk. paper)
        I. Alter-Gilbert, Gilbert.    II. Title.    III. Series: Discoveries.
    PQ7797.L85 F813 2001
    863.62--dc21                                                00-5560
                                                                        CIP

Cover illustration: *The Visionary* by Jerry Wayne Downs, courtesy of the David
Clark collection and Diane Nelson Fine Art, Laguna Beach, California

The Paper used in this publication meets the minimum requirements of the
American National Standard for Performance of Paper for Printed Library
Materials Z39.48-1984

Latin American Literary Review Press
121 Edgewood Ave.
Pittsburgh, PA 15218

NATIONAL
ENDOWMENT
FOR THE ARTS

*Acknowledgments*
This project is supported in part
by grants from the
National Endowment for the Arts in Washington D.C.,
a federal agency,
and the
Commonwealth of Pennsylvania
Council on the Arts.

PENNSYLVANIA
COUNCIL
ON THE
ARTS

# ~CONTENTS~

# *Foreword*

Anyone chancing upon the prim figure of Leopoldo Lugones on the streets of Buenos Aires during the 1930s might understandably mistake him for a diplomat or an officer of a bank. The moon-faced gent, regally erect, with his starched collar, derby hat, spectacles and spats, had the air of a particularly priggish schoolmaster and was more likely to be taken for a crabbed government functionary than a lion of Latin American letters. But Lugones was just such a lion, a living legend wreathed in controversy, a protean artist who tore through the Argentinian intellectual landscape like a force of nature in an epic career lasting three decades and yielding forty-two books, a dozen pamphlets, and several hundred miscellaneous articles and essays. From his superbly rational brain flowed polemical tracts, critical analyses, and historical commentaries, while his extra-fecund imagination produced haunting poetry, atmospheric, quasi-mystical novels, and disturbing tales of lacerating nightmare. Beneath his staid exterior dwelt the complex personality of a man aseethe with passion, always in the public eye, the subject of diatribe and dithyramb, whose name was both dragged through the mud and flung amongst the stars. Cultural crusader and political paladin, he was a man of combat, always at war with prevailing orthodoxy. He could be as dogmatic and contentious as he was valiant and generous, and inspired equal doses of ire and admiration, vilification and veneration. Abuzz with contradictions, he was an amateur Arabic scholar who became deeply involved in national politics at the highest levels, an erudite Hellenist who was at one time an anti-clerical, anti-Spanish anarchist, a radical socialist, a democrat, an intolerant reactionary right-wing extremist and apologist for oligarchy and military rule, and a walking repository of a dozen branches of knowledge who suffered in silence the secret agony of tortured love. Public poet, esteemed figurehead, militant defender of the values of the nation, he was a cosmopolitan thinker bound on a restless, lifelong quest for an elusive Absolute, whose tempestuous spiritual itinerary would carry him through more phases than a calendar has moons. A professional wild card, revered by friend and feared by foe, the force of his tumultous will propelled him through a life every bit as baroque as his writing style could be.

Lugones regularly took practice in the fencing academy at the Military School in Buenos Aires. A romantic, a gallant, and a devotee of the chivalric code, he once fought a duel with a colonel and challenged the young poet Jorge Luis Borges to another when he felt insulted by what he considered a slight in the newspapers; the contest wasn't consummated on account of Borges' blindness about which, when he learned of it, Lugones said, "In that case, please be so kind as to inform that lackey Borges that he would do well not to make unsubstantiated assertions in the newspapers which he is not prepared to defend with his person." The lackey Borges would later write an adulatory book about his challenger.

Lugones was constantly denigrated and maligned because of his political vacillations. Although he undertook each shift of ideology with utmost sincerity, he was inflexibly doctrinaire. His son felt compelled to author a book titled *The Enemies of Lugones*, so plentiful were they, apparently. He was called everything from "civilized monster" to "systematic bore". Even Georges Clemenceau, the Tiger of France, called Lugones a "terror". Lugones was all these things and more, yet so great a force in shaping the cultural landscape of his cherished homeland that he became a national myth.

Leopoldo Lugones was born in the city of Córdoba, Argentina in 1874, where his privileged family had been settled for centuries, some of his ancestors having been conquistadors. He was a child prodigy, "born superannuated"; an aristocrat whose formal education extended to secondary school, from which he dropped out in a fit of rebellious pique during his teens, but whose native intelligence and cultivation by private tutors enabled him to flower into one of the leading Latin American intellectuals of the twentieth century, and a poet generally considered one of the greatest in the Spanish language. He was histrionic, vain, and precocious from infancy. While a child he announced to his illustrious grandfather, a military hero of the republic, "You are the savior of our race; I am its poet. You have the sword, I have the pen." Lugones' escutcheon would always be emblazoned with both eagle and nightingale, for country and beauty were his two grand passions. After completing *The Worlds*, his first work of verse, the sixteen-year old patriot-aesthete continued his independent study of Nietzche, Bakunin, Zola, and Tolstoy, became a distinguished pedagogue and, less than fifteen years later, Argentina's Superintendent of Instruction and Inspector of Schools, in which capacity he distinguished himself by introducing enlightened initiatives and bold reforms. He enjoyed a long, accomplished career as a high-ranking government administrator holding a number of posts, including the assistant postmaster generalship and the directorship of the National Teachers Library. His functions in officialdom were combined with his activities as a freemason, a prison reformer, a strike organizer, a supporter of Dreyfus, an educator, archivist, editor of avant-garde reviews, philosopher, and scientist.

By 1892, Lugones was reading his poems in theatrical arenas, beginning what was to become a lifetime of lecturing and public speaking as one of Argentina's noblest and most sought-after orators. A stirring rhetorician who lent his talent to both aesthetic and political causes, Lugones could be seen, decades before Juan and Eva Peron stepped onto the stage of Argentine history with their own brand of fiery oratory, going the rounds of club, veranda, and athenaeum, holding forth in his baritone, clear and sonorous voice, a lord of elocution.

In his late teens, one of his former teachers described Lugones as "a red radical, a subversive, and an incendiary". By the age of twenty-one, he had become involved in anarcho-socialist activities; even the likes of his lifelong friend, the august Nicaraguan poet Ruben Dario characterized him in an article as a revolutionary as much as a poet.

With Rubén Darío and José Ingenieros, he formed the humorist-esoteric sect *Syrinx* and, in 1896, he installed himself permanently in Buenos Aires, where he took up journalism partly as a means of livelihood and partly to try his wings as a writer. Throughout his life, he considered himself a journalist, even after he was hailed as an internationally consecrated intellectual. He wrote on an unheard of variety of themes, not as a dilettante but as a master of them all. In 1903, he went on an archaeological expedition in Misiones province with Uruguayan writer Horacio Quiroga acting as photographer; they lived in the jungle studying ruins of Jesuit missions, which resulted in the book *Jesuit Empire*. He was a *modernista*, a member of an international assimilationist movement quite different in aims and purposes from the *tropicalismo* movement which was to come later, but Lugones was a pre-tropicalismo tropicalista in that he championed all things Spanish American, especially Argentinian.

The course of Lugones' spiritual evolution was every bit as meandering and mercurial as the stream of his political thought, and was paralleled, to a pronounced degree, by trends in his writing. During adolescence, he was caught up in a sort of juvenile paganism which took the form of pantheistic nature-worship, and he insisted that "the gods haven't died and they're going to return"; antichristian hellenism was upstaged by a cosmogonic philosophy embracing an anthroposophist type of "science of man"; both were eventually replaced by positivism and a final Catholic synthesis, when the seeker reverted to his roots. Initiated at an early age in spiritism, theosophy, magic, and other elements of the esoteric tradition, the prolific poet lent his plume to the propagation of such verse works as *The Book of Landscapes*; *Garden of Evening*; *Moonstricken*; and *Gilded Hours*; and to the short stories contained in *Fatal Tales* as well as the novel, *The Angel of Darkness*, and *Philosophicules*, a compendium of philosophical fables. The precepts of animism espoused by theosophy and related systems provided the young adept with the metaphysical equipage and metaphorical palette to forge exquisite impressionistic poems of a Symbolist-Decadent stripe, followed by pastoral impressionist poetry of a high order. All Lugones' early poetry is marked by elegance and preciosity of diction. His lexical extravagance, his verbal coloratura borders on grandiloquence. Because of the sensuality of his imagery, Lugones was called " a flagellant of vice" and his work "profane, erotic, drowning in a delicious panic of sin". It was also said to be full of "subtle siftings, crepuscular harmonies, whinings and swoonings, slow macerations of desire and painful awakenings". Like so many others, from Byron to Huidobro, Lugones regarded the poet's role as that of prophet and oracle, and he also held the view that the poet should be a leader of men in their struggle for a more just society.

When the Great War broke out in 1914, Lugones adopted a pro-democracy position but after the armistice, disillusioned with what he considered the stagnation of postwar society, turned against parliamentarianism and politicians and, impressed with Mussolini, took up the Fascist cause, which he perceived as a purifier and redeemer of spent ideas, exhausted creeds, and the decadent moral laxity of the interbellum period. After the First World War, Lugones felt that Christian civilization, founded on the cult of death and the adoration of blood, which was reproduced daily with the propitiatory victim of its own God "actually present" through transubstantiation of the eucharist, found in the war its natural conclusion. There was nothing surprising to Lugones about the masses, caught up in the traumatic European conflict, hurling themselves into the pillage of civilization. France named him a chevalier in the Legion of Honor in 1921. By 1922, Lugones had become anti-democratic, and began making speeches condemning the oppobrium of politicians as a race, and the Argentine press went berserk, acrimoniously attacking his latest change in political orientation. He became a staunch nationalist and began to pal around with military cabals. In 1924, he gave his notorious "Hour of the Sword" speech, which sent shock waves throughout the South American continent, when he touted a strong military as a final bastion against "demagogic dissolution". Don Leopoldo was soon befriending the Argentine oligarchs and consorting with conspiratorial army officers in the Jockey Club. When

General José Uriburu came to power in the Argentine coup of 1930, Lugones drafted Uriburu's proclamation of authority and gave a funeral address for the cadets killed during the takeover. Nevertheless, Lugones declined the directorship of the National Library when it was extended to him in acknowledgment of his support.

Late in life, while still observing a respectable domesticity with his wife of many years, Lugones conceived a profoundly impassioned and tragically frustrated love for Emilia Cadelago, whom he met when he was in his early fifties and she in her twenties. He called this "immortal girl" Aglaura, after the Greek goddess of the same name, and he loved her "to the point of paroxysm". His son threatened to file for a certification of insanity and have Lugones committed to a mental institution, if he didn't cut off the affair. The intimidated girl conceded to the conservative social strictures of the day, rebuffed the tortured poet, and refused all further communication. Despite her ardent suitor's earnest entreaties in the form of "painfully erotic letters" and bouquets of verse brimming with castles and princesses, flowers and swans, Aglaura's renunciation was total. Lugones looked for her constantly when he passed the Martial Circle on his way to The Frond, but he never saw her again. Bereft of his beloved Aglaura, relegated to a state of political and ideological ridicule, at first hated and reviled, then consigned to indifference, Lugones was driven mad by disgust and contempt, and committed suicide in 1938 by ingesting cyanide at the resort of Tiger Island, near Buenos Aires.

Of Lugones' lasting legacy of epochal and innovative literary works, perhaps the most original and memorable is the 1906 masterpiece of fantastic fiction, *Strange Forces*. Though quite a chimera when it made its debut, this suite of short stories accompanied by a systematic cosmological essay did not arise from a vacuum. Gaslamp Era science fiction, represented by such writers as Jules Verne and H. G. Wells, was already well established. Contemporaneous with *Strange Forces* was the speculative fiction of Jack London and Arthur Conan Doyle and, just around the corner, the rash of early twentieth century adventure fantasy and sword-and-sorcery sagas featuring such characters as Tarzan, Peter Pan, and Conan the Cimmerian, created by the likes of Sir James Barrie, Edgar Rice Burroughs, Arthur Machen, and Robert E. Howard.

Science allegory and horror literature with paranormal themes had become standard fare in such nineteenth century literary offerings as Robert Louis Stevenson's *Dr. Jekyll and Mr. Hyde*; Mary Shelley's *Frankenstein*; de Maupassant's *The Horla*; Hawthorne's *Rappacinni's Daughter*; Bram Stoker's *Dracula*; and in the ghost stories of Sheridan Le Fanu and the gothic tales of Edgar Allan Poe. The works of the German Romantics such as E.T.A. Hoffmann and Adelbert von Chamisso, who so influenced Poe, also, no doubt, influenced Lugones' own forerunners in the long and rich tradition of Argentine fantastic literature. Lugones' friend and mentor Eduardo Holmberg had authored an excellent collection of fantastic tales as early as 1870. Other Argentine predecessors include Miguel Cané, Juana Manuela Gorriti, Eduardo Wilde, Carlos Olivera, Carlos Monsálve, and Carlos Octavio Bunge. All were crafting outstanding tales of horror, fantasy, and science fiction well in advance of the appearance of *Strange Forces*. Lugones, in turn, would set a pattern for all the practitioners of imaginative fiction to follow, consciously or unconsciously exerting influence on Jorge Luis Borges, Julio Cortázar, and others down through Luisa Valenzuela, Fernando Sorrentino, and Ana Maria Shua. The difference between Lugones and other authors in this line was that for Lugones, his notions of supernatural operations and secret forces were not merely framing devices or dramatic pretexts on which to hang his stories, but actual verities; confirmed truths to which he wholeheartedly subscribed.

*Strange Forces* was composed not only in the spirit of the new science erupting at the end of the nineteenth century and the beginning of the twentieth, but was, more importantly, governed by a sense of life's mystery; in its pages, apocalyptic catastrophes, wars, panics, and biblical curses unfold under attenuated light, and give expression to Lugones' dark "cosmovision". In the 1890s Lugones was reading, on the one hand, Cuvier, Lamarck, Darwin, Haeckel and Spencer and, on the other, Madame Blavatsky. Lugones' first volume of verse, written in 1890 when he was sixteen, and probably having as its muse the French astronomer-philosopher Camille

Flammarion, was cosmological in theme: *The Worlds*. Fantastic literature was quite the vogue in turn-of-the-century Buenos Aires, and a fascination with the paranormal took the form of participation in seances, ouija parties, consultations with clairvoyants, and the study of the cabala. It was the era of Tesla and Edison, the age of the cannon rather than intercontinental ballistic missiles. Scientific fantasy speculated, with a mixture of awe and fear, on bold new worlds to come, at a time when science was crossing thresholds never before crossed by man. Taking his cue from these preoccupations, Lugones dextrously appropriated the most advanced ideas from the frontiers of chemistry, biology, and physics, and interblended them with hermetic doctrines and popular lore concerning such phenomena as zoanthropic metamorphoses, vampire plants, doppelgangers, and bilocation, all delivered in an informative tone lending credence to the proceedings, and unified by a single underlying principle: that when man tampers with the natural order of things and dares to reach for knowledge of things which God did not intend man to know, he must invariably suffer punishment.

In the story *The Omega Force*, the apparatus dissolves the brain of its inventor; in *Metamusic*, the investigator is left blind after finding the octave of the sun; in *Psychon*, he is driven mad after liberating liquid thought. These stories log the laboratory mishaps of scientists deranged by obsessive fixation. Some of these mad scientists are perverse or malign, motivated by grief and resentment or desire for revenge; others quest after secret knowledge hitherto concealed. But they are all sustained by the same impetus that drives the monk Pipistratus in *The Pillar of Salt*: none is able to resist the temptation to penetrate into hidden mysteries whose prohibition is divinely ordained. Neither God nor Nature will tolerate violations of these mandates and designs and, with Olympian indifference, an iron heel crushes all transgressors.

Lugones authored other fantastic stories both before and after the period of *Strange Forces*. Some of them are about madmen, others about people who are haunted; often his scientists are mad or half-mad with obsession in their doomed quests after Lost Chords and Ultimate Ground. *In The Negative Mirror*, which object acts as a psychic inductor in an experiment gone awry, yet another scientist can be found on a doomed, extralimitary quest. Nonscientists, as in *Luisa Frascati*, are haunted by bewitching females. In this respect, Lugones seems to have taken to heart Poe's assertion that there is no more fitting subject for poetry than the death of a beautiful woman. Still other stories focus on the fixations of lunatics: In *The Discovery of the Circumference*, an asylum inmate insists that stepping outside the chalk circle which circumscribes him will spell mortal peril; In *The Definitive*, another inmate is at first ignored in disbelief when he claims he is being stalked by a power he calls "the Definitive"; in *The Ultimate Blunder*, a maniac tries to snatch the sun from the heavens, as if he were picking an apple; in *The Dead Man*, the town cuckoo wanders the streets professing to be dead; in *Hipalia*, a young woman spends all day and night staring at a blank wall in an attempt to project her own image onto it and, when she finishes the task, dies. Lugones also had a penchant for animal stories, of which some of the best are *The Scrawny Dog*; *The Old Cat*; and *The Concept of Death*. His forays in the genre of the conte cruel include *The Final Shot* and *A Case of Illogic* while *Nuralkamar* is an example of his skill with the oriental romance. Additionally, he penned "fatal" tales such as *The Dagger* and just plain perplexing tales such as *The Man in the Tree* .

In the purely quizzical fictions, as well as those of damnation and foredoom and hopeless endings, there is a common denominator: all of them revolve around situations in which the irrational plane invades the rational; it's as if Lugones were warning that mankind, in its restless curiosity, may open one door too many and, like Pandora, unleash strange forces of destruction which can no longer be contained. The prescience with which Lugones anticipated the destructive potential of science decades before the dawn of the Atomic Age, as well as his recognition of mankind's sad moral frailty, accredits him no less a prophet than Verne or Wells. Nearly one hundred years after they were written, these coruscating tales owe their enduring power to a mind which wrought them with a nobility of conception, vividness of construction, and lyricism in the telling only a true poet could bring to bear. But more significantly still, remains

# The Firestorm

INVOCATION OF A DISEMBODIED SPIRIT OF GOMORRAH

*And I will make your heaven as iron and your earth as brass.*
— Leviticus XXVI, 19

*I* remember that it was a beautiful sunny day, with crowds bustling in streets choked with vehicles. A blithely warm day, sublime, perfect.

From my terrace dominating a vast confusion of roofs overgrown with fruits and flowers and tangled vines, could be seen a stretch of the lakeshore flecked with trees, the gray strip of an arcaded avenue…

Just before eleven the first cinders fell. One here, one there…copper chips resembling sparks from a torch; incandescent particles of copper which struck the pavement with a little whishing hiss, like granules of spilled sand. The sky was as clear as ever; the urban underdrone didn't diminish. Only the birds in my aviary stopped singing.

Gradually I began to notice it while gazing at the horizon in a moment of abstraction. At first I thought it was an optical illusion brought on by my myopia. I seemed to wait a long time before seeing another cinder fall, because the sunlight overpowered them in brightness, but the copper blazed in such a way that the burning particles distinctly defined themselves, even when bathed by the solar rays. Then a jagged virgule of fire streaked across the sky like a diagonal whiplash, and made a craterlet in the earth. Others followed, at long intervals.

I must confess that I was beginning to experience a vague terror. I scanned the sky with an anxious glance. It was still clear. Where was this strange hail coming from? What kind of copper was this? Was it copper at all?

Then, a few feet away from me, a cinder fell on my terrace. I stooped to pick it up; it was, there could be no doubt, a minute nugget of copper which was very slow to cool. Fortunately, a breeze came up, deflecting this singular rain onto the opposite side of my terrace. The cinders were quite fine, alright. At any minute, I had thought the phenomenon was going to stop. It didn't stop. The particles were falling one by one, that was certain, but in ever larger lumps.

Although normally, nothing would have kept me from having my breakfast, it was now noon. I headed downstairs towards the dining-room, crossing the garden, not without a certain trepidation about the cinders. Then I remembered that the awning shielding the pathway from the sun would shelter me...

Shelter me? I swiveled my eyes; the awning was riddled with tiny pores, almost too tiny to be noticed.

In the dining room I awaited an admirable breakfast; my fortunate celibacy prized two things above all: reading and eating. Except for my library, the dining room was my pride. Sick of women and a little gouty, where amiable vices were concerned all else could wait except gluttony. I ate alone, while a slave read me travel narratives. Never had I been able to comprehend the practice of taking meals in company; and if I disliked women, as I have told you, you can imagine how I abhorred men.

It had been ten years since my last orgy! Since then, busying myself with my gardens, my fish, my birds, I simply had no time to go out. Sometimes, on hot afternoons, I went for a stroll along the shore of the lake. It pleased me to look at it, decorated by the moon at night, but that was all, and I spent months without frequenting it.

The vast libertine city was for me a desert where my pleasures found asylum. A few friends; brief visits; long hours at table; lectures; my fish, my birds; an occasional evening of entertainment by a troupe of flutists, and two or three attacks of gout per year...

I had the honor of being consulted for banquets and, I suppose it's fair to say, I was not without celebrity for two or three sauces of my invention. This entitled me - and I say this without conceit - to a municipal bust, with just as much reason as any one of my compatriots who had invented a new kind of kiss.

Well, as I was saying, my slave read to me. As I ate, he read narratives about the sea and the snow, which admirably augmented the generous coolness of the amphorae in setting the mood for my ensuing nap. Perhaps the rain of fire had ceased, I thought, since the servant gave no indication of having noticed it.

Suddenly the slave, who was crossing the garden with another platter, couldn't suppress a scream. He came, nevertheless, to the table; but his lividity attested to a horrible pain. He had in his naked shoulder a little hole, at the bottom of which sizzled the voracious ember which had bored it. I instructed him to bathe it with oil and salve, and sent him to bed where his groans continued unabated.

This brusquely curtailed my appetite; and though I continued to poke at the dishes so as not to demoralize my servant, something inside me struggled to understand. The incident had left me disconcerted.

It was halfway through my nap hour when I went up again onto the terrace. The ground was strewn with copper granules, but the rain didn't seem to be increasing. I had just begun to be calmed by this thought, when a new wave of disquiet swept over me. The silence was absolute. All traffic had come to a halt, because of the phenomenon, no doubt. There was not so much as a whisper in the city. Only, from time to time, a faint murmur of wind among the trees. There was also something very disturbing about the behavior of my birds. They had bunched together in a corner almost one on top of the other. I was stirred by compassion and decided to open the door to let them out. They wouldn't budge; instead, they huddled together with even more vexation than before. It was then that the idea of impending cataclysm began to seep in with all its intimidations.

Though my scientific erudition wasn't great, I knew that no one had ever mentioned such rains of incandescent copper. Copper rains! The air contains no copper mines. Later the limpidity of the sky left no conjecture about their derivation. And this was the most alarming thing about the phenomenon. The cinders came from everywhere and nowhere. An invisible immensity was crumbling into fire. The terrible copper fell from the firmament; but the firmament remained imperturbably blue. There stole over me bit by bit a strange dismay, an unsettling wave of consternation; but, rare thing: until then I hadn't thought of fleeing. This idea was mixed with disagreeable associations. Flight! And my table, my books, my birds, my fish which had just begun to flourish, my gardens already ennobled by antiquity, my fifty years of placidity, lived in the deliciousness of the moment, without a care for the morrow...

Flee? And I thought with horror of my possessions (which hadn't been packed) on the other side of the desert, with their camel drivers sleeping in tents of coarse black wool and taking for their total nourishment curdled milk, toasted bulgar, soured honey...

I wandered in a fugue down by the lake, escaping only briefly, as it turned out, since on the lake, as on the desert, it was also raining copper; and the rain, since it had no discernible focus, must have been general.

In spite of the vague terror which seized me, I reasoned all this with poise and lucidity, discussing it calmly with myself, though a little unnerved, to tell the truth, by the digestive lethargy which invariably accompanied my afternoon nap. And something told me that the phenomenon was not going to pass. Just the same, I decided, there was nothing to lose by preparing a cart.

At this moment, the air was filled with a vast vibration of bells. And almost simultaneously, I noticed something: it was no longer raining copper. The pealing was an act of thanks, a joyous dance of relief accompanied by the sing-song undertone of the reanimating city. It was waking from its fleeting astonishment, doubly garrulous. In some districts bombs were still burning.

Leaning over the railing of the terrace, I gazed down with a baffled sense of well being, becoming one with the vespertinal commotion which was all love and luxury. The sky remained clear. Solicitous boys painstakingly gathered in bowls the copper ingots, which the metalsmiths and junkmen had begun to sell. This was all that was left of the great celestial menace.

More numerous than ever, the people of pleasure crammed the streets, and I remember that I smiled vaguely at one equivocal young man, whose tunic was hitched up around his hips as he took a leap across the mouth of a street, affording me a glimpse of his smooth legs, striped with ribbons. Courtesans, their breasts uncovered as had become the latest fashion, and thrust forward by dazzling corsets, luxuriated in their indolence, perspiring heady perfumes. An old pander enthroned on his chariot flapped, as though it were a veil, a tin leaf covering a large leather portfolio, from which he intermittently revealed pictures depicting monstrous loves: conjunctions of lizards with swans; the union of a monkey and a seal; a young girl covered by the jeweled delirium of a peacock. A beautiful album, of the rarest quality, he assured me, and guaranteed the authenticity of the pieces. Animals subdued by who knows what barbarous methods, and disoriented with opium and asafetida.

Followed by three young men in masquerade, there wriggled past a lovely negress who, while dispensing colored powders to the rhythm of a dance, drew on the sidewalks a rare selection of secret scenes. They knew how to dye hair using orpiment, and offered to paint fingernails.

A spongy personage, whose condition of eunuchhood could be divined in his morbidity, extolled, to the sound of a brass rattle, the virtues of blankets made from a unique fabric which produced insomnia and desire. Blankets whose abolition had been petitioned by the more upright citizens. But my city knew how to enjoy, how to live!

That evening I received two visitors who dined with me. A jovial condisciple, a mathematician whose disordered and irregular life was the scandal of science, and a wealthy planter. People felt the need to socialize after the rain of those copper cinders. We visited and drank, then both went to bed completely drunk. I made a hasty exit. The city, capriciously illuminated, was celebrating its deliverance from the crisis by hurling itself into a night of festivity. From darkened alcoves shone the light of incense burners and scented lamps. From their balconies, young women, excessively embellished, diverted themselves by blowing projectiles from their noses onto distracted passersby, and making razzing noises by venting air from painted bladders and shaking rattles and strings of tiny bells. On every corner there was dancing. From balcony to balcony they exchanged flowers and sweet cakes. The lawns of the parks teemed with couples...

After awhile, I turned around and went home. Never did I climb into bed with more gratitude for the heaviness of dreams.

I woke bathed in sweat, my eyes turbid, my throat dry. Outside, was the rumor of rain. Bumbling out of bed, I felt for the wall, and a shiver of fear ran along my body like the flail of a whip. The wall was hot and pulsing with a mute vibration. It was scarcely necessary to open the window to realize what had happened.

The rain of copper had returned, but this time the pellets were fat and dense. A caliginous vapor suffocated the city; a smell somewhere between that of phosphate and urine empested the air. Luckily, my house was surrounded by galleries and this rain couldn't reach the doors.

I opened the one that gave on the garden. The trees were black, divested of foliage; the ground was littered with carbonized leaves. The air, zigzagged by virgules of fire, was in a state of mortal paralysis; and all the while, the firmament, serene, unperturbed, radiated celestial composure.

I called, I shouted in vain. The rain had penetrated even the servants quarters, and the servant had been in there. I wrapped my legs in a nacre blanket, and armored my shoulders and head with a metal bath tub - which pinched me horribly - so as to be able to get to the stables. The horses had also disappeared. And with a tranquility which did honor to my nerves, I told myself that all was lost.

The larder, however, was still amply stocked; the cellar brimming with wines. I went down to have a look. Everything had kept its freshness;

down in the subterranean vault, the vibration of the heavy rain didn't reach, nor did the echo of its grave crepitation. I drank a bottle, and later I drew from a secret cupboard the pomander of poison wine. Everyone who owned a wine cellar had one, though no one ever used it, even on the most obnoxious of guests. It was a clear, tasteless liquid, instantaneous in effect.

Revived by the wine, I examined my situation. It was simple enough. I couldn't escape, death awaited me; but with the poison, death belonged to me. And I decided to see all it might be possible to see, of what promised, undoubtedly, to be a singular spectacle. A downpour of incandescent copper! The city in flames! To experience such a sight was worth any amount of trouble.

I climbed upstairs, intending to go onto the terrace, but I couldn't get through the door which gave access to it. From where I stood, I could see enough, however. I watched and I listened. The solitude was absolute. The crepitation was uninterrupted except by one after another howling dog, or unnatural explosion. The entire environs glowed red, and strewn everywhere were tree trunks, chimneys, whole houses blanched by a woeful pallor. The few trees that still had any branches were twisted around themselves, and blasted black as lead. The light had lessened somewhat, in spite of the persistence of the celestial limpidity. The horizon was now much closer, and as if suffocated by ash. Over the lake floated a thick vapor, which somehow mitigated the extraordinary dryness of the air.

I clearly perceived, in the combustible rain, prodigious skeins of copper hunks which vibrated like innumerable harp strings interspersed with the fizzle of random flamelets. Black smoke announced the impact of incendiaries here and there.

My birds began to perish from thirst and I tried to go down to nurse them by bringing them water. The cellar communicated with a large cistern which could resist a great deal of celestial fire but some copper, emptying from the gutters and drains of the roof and the patios, had already slipped in, and the water had a peculiar taste, between natron and urine, when I tried to swallow it. This impelled me to put in place the mosaic lids which shut off certain conduits and passageways and cut my water from communication with the outside.

That afternoon and all that night a horrendous spectacle engulfed the city. Incinerated in their domiciles, the people had all but vanished. Vaporized in their beds, roasted in the streets, enkindled in the fields, they agonized barbarically with yowls and shrieks of a stupendous amplitude, horror, and variety. There is nothing quite so sublime as the human voice. The collapse of edifices, the combustion of diverse goods and merchandise and, more than anything else, the conflagration of so many bodies, added to the cataclysm the misery of an infernal stench. When the sun went down, the air was almost black with smoke and dust clouds. The flamelets which danced the first morning of the storm, now were sinister fireballs. A dense, ardent wind began to blow, filling the air with something like the fumes given off by hot pitch. It seemed as if everything was turning into an immense dark oven. Sky, earth, air: everything was caught up. There was nothing but shadows and fire. Ah, the horror of those shadows which all the enormous fire of the broiling city could not quite dominate; and the fetor of rags, of sulfur, of cadaverous grease in the dry air which had spit blood; and those screams that couldn't possibly accomplish anything, those screams rising above the noise of the firestorm, vaster than a hurricane, those groans and wailings, and those growlings and bellowings of all the dumb beasts howling with an ineffable dread of eternity!...

I made my way down to the cistern still without having lost my presence of mind, although thoroughly electrified by all this horror; suddenly I found myself in a friendly darkness and, as I surrendered to the refuge of the coolness and the assuaging silence of the subterranean water, I was overtaken by a sort of fear I hadn't felt - of this I am sure - for forty years or more: the infantile fear of a diffuse enemy presence; and I broke down and started weeping, started sobbing like a madman, sobbing with fright, there in a corner, without any shame.

It wasn't much later when I heard the roof cave in and, immediately after it came crashing down, I went to barricade the cellar door. I did this with its own ladder, and some barrels which had been stacked against one wall, and the erection of this defense afforded me some comfort; it couldn't have saved me, but it made me feel better to try to do something, and the effort itself had a beneficial effect. As I intermittently dropped off into drowsiness cut short by dismal nightmares, the hours passed. I continued to hear the sporadic concussions of the ongoing downfall all around outside. I lit two lamps I had brought with me, to give myself courage, since the cellar was extremely murky. I even managed to eat, though without appetite, the remainder of a pie. On the other hand, I drank a great deal of water.

Suddenly my lamps began to flicker, and true terror, a numbing terror this time, clutched me in its iron fist. I had wasted, without foreseeing it, all my light, since I hadn't thought, when I descended that afternoon, to bring more with me.

The lamps burned low and snuffled out. Then I noticed that the cellar was beginning to fill up with the stench of the firestorm. There was no recourse but to vacate; and anything, anything was preferable to dying asphyxiated like a savage in his cave.

I had scarcely unbarred the cellar's hatch before smoldering fragments from the larder covered it...

For the second time the infernal fire had stopped. But the city no longer existed. Roofs, doors, most of the walls, all the towers, were already in ruins. The silence was colossal; a veritably catastrophic silence. Five or six huge smoke rings billowed above the peaks; and underneath a limpid, bland, sublimely tranquil sky - a sky whose blue simplicity attested to eternal indifferences - sprawled the poor city, dead, dead forever, stinking like a veritable cadaver.

The singularity of the situation, the enormity of the phenomenon and, without doubt, the satisfaction of having found myself, alone amongst the populace, the only person to have been preserved, dulled the pain of my suffering, and replaced it with a somber curiosity. The archway of my entrance hall still was standing, and I sat down in the hollow of its columns, which remained intact all the way to the imposts.

Everything flammable was gone, and what was left looked like a vulcan's forge, strewn with spelt and slag and scoria. In places the ash hadn't covered, the simmering tokens of the metallic rain shone with vermilion fire. It gave the desert floor the resplendence of a sandbox of glowing copper. Over the mountains on the far side of the lake, the vaporized waters condensed to produce a massive udder of moisture and it was this which had kept the air breathable during the cataclysm. The sun was shining intensely and this solitude began to oppress me with a profound sense of desolation, when I made out, through the smoke and dust enshrouding my doorway, a silhouette wandering among the ruins. It was a man, and he had certainly seen me, for he was moving in my direction.

It didn't seem in the least strange when he came and, stepping under the arch, sat down with me. I took him for a boatman, saved, like me, by a cellar, but where he was being punished by his master. He had been able to flood the cellar with the cistern water, and by that means escape.

Assured in this respect, I began to interrogate him. All the boats had gone up in flames, as well as the mills, and the mines. The lake had turned bitter. Although I noticed we were speaking in lowered voices, it never occurred to me - I have no idea why - to raise mine.

I offered him the run of my cellar, where two dozen hams were left, some cheeses, all the wine…

All of a sudden we noticed a cloud of dust along the edge of the desert. The dust of a chariot? Some party sent, perhaps, to bring assistance to the compatriots of Adama or Seboim?

Soon we were forced to abandon this hope in deference to a spectacle as desolate as it was dangerous.

It was a troop of lions, the fierce survivors of the desert, which had repaired to the city as if it were an oasis, furious with thirst, crazed by the cataclysm.

Thirst and not hunger infuriated them, since they passed by without noticing us. And in that state they circled and circled. Nothing revealed the lugubriousness of the catastrophe as revealingly as they.

Bald as mangy cats, their manes reduced to pitiful wisps of singed strands, their flanks seared unevenly, giving them the comic disproportion of half-clothed clowns wearing oversized masks, their tails standing on end and twitching, like those of rats in flight, their pustulous paws, dribbling blood - all this declared in the clearest terms their three days of horror beneath the celestial lash, at the mercy of the insecure dens which proved unable to protect them.

They prowled the dry precincts with a human derangement in their eyes, abruptly meandering from extinguished well to extinguished well; until finally they sat down in the dust, dropping onto their haunches, blistered muzzles in the air, eyes glazed over in a wandering stare filled with desolation and with eternity, questioning the sky, I am sure of it, as they started to roar with unendurable abjection.

Ah…nothing, not the cataclysm with its horrors, nor the clamor of the moribund city was so horrific as this lament of the beasts atop the ruins. Those roars had contained evidence of speech. They cried with who knows what unconscious and deserted sorrows, to some obscure divinity. In the succinct souls of the beasts the fear of the incomprehensible was added to the terrors of death. If everything else remained the same, the daily sun, the eternal sky, the familiar desert, why was everything burning up and why was there no water…? And lacking any idea whatever of the relationship of these phenomena, their horror was blind, which is to say, even more frightful. The conveyance of their pain was elevated by a certain vague notion of forethought, before that sky from which the infernal rain had been falling; and their plaintive roars unmistakably asked what tremendous thing had been the cause of their affliction. Ah…those roars, the only aspect of grandeur kept by these diminished brutes: what a comment on the secret horror of the catastrophe; what an interpretation of the irremediable pain of eternal solitude, eternal silence, eternal thirst…

But all this lasted but a short while. The candent metal began to rain again, denser, heavier, than ever.

In our hasty descent we were able to see that the beasts disbanded looking for shelter under the rubble.

We got to the cellar, not without being caught by some of the cinders; and when I comprehended that this new shower was going to consume what was left, I determined to end it all.

As my companion pillaged the cellar - for the first and last time, to be sure - I decided to sample the cistern water preparatory to taking my funeral bath and, after hunting unsuccessfully for a slice of ham, I climbed into it by the little ladder which was used to inspect its purity, and keep it clean.

Having brought the poison pomander, which gave me a great sense of well-being, I was barely bothered by curiosity about death.

The fresh water and the darkness turned my thoughts to the voluptuosities of my wealthy existence which was about to come to an end. Plunging up to my neck, I was overwhelmed by the exhilaration of the cleanness and a gentle sensation of comfortable domesticity managed to soothe me.

I heard the hurricane of fire outside. Chunks of rubble had once again begun to fall. From the cellar not a whisper leaked. I perceived a reflection of the flames which were flickering through the cellar door, the tell-tale urine-smell of the brimstone…I lifted the pomander to my lips, and…

# An Inexplicable Phenomenon

*It's* been eleven years now. I had been traveling through the agricultural region dividing the provinces of Cordoba and Santa Fe, forearmed with the indispensable warnings to avoid the atrocious inns prevalent throughout these developing colonies. My stomach was in a perpetual state of upset from the inevitable stews garnished with fennel and the lethal walnut desserts which comprised the fundamental refections. This latest peregrination must have gone into effect under bad auspices. No one could direct me to a hostel in the town to which I had been headed. I was pressed to the point of desperation, when the justice of the peace, professing a certain sympathy for me, came to my aid.

"I know a place," he said to me. "It belongs to a widower who lives there by himself. He owns the house, the best in the colony, and various tracts of land of no particular value. Certain notarial services I recently performed for him have put me in his good graces, and this would make a happy pretext for furnishing you, if you like, with a letter of introduction, which will guarantee that you will be received with the warmest hospitality. I'm sure you'll find the lodgings most comfortable and in every way suitable to your needs. If such an arrangement appeals to you, just bear in mind that the man in question, his finer qualities notwithstanding, is a bit on the eccentric side, though extraordinarily reserved. No one has been able to penetrate any part of his house beyond the suite of bedrooms where he installs his guests, who are very few, from the look of it. Not that any of this is terribly important, but I felt I ought to tell you, in any case. Make of it what you will. This said, if you wish a letter of introduction,…"

I accepted gratefully and, tucking this document in my coat pocket, continued my journey, arriving at my destination several hours later.

Nothing about the place was attractive. There was the station with its roof of colored tiles, its creaking platform coated with coal dust, its semaphore to the right, its water tank to the left. On the tracks, stood a half dozen freight cars carrying the harvest in their hoppers. In the background, peeped the railroad workers' shack, hemmed in by bundles of wheat. Level with the roadbed was the pampa with its yellowish color like that of herbal tea; tiny houses lacking whitewash were sprinkled in the distance, each with its unthrashed corn stacked outside; squiggled along the horizon was a festoon of smoke streaming from a speeding train and, over everything, hung an enormously peaceful silence which complimented the rural colors of the landscape.

This was vulgarly symmetrical like all the fresh construction. Surveyors' lines could be seen bisecting the physiognomy of the autumnal prairie. When some of the colonists came to the express office to collect their mail, I asked one of them about the house in question, and immediately obtained directions. I noticed, from the way everyone referred to my host, that the latter was taken for a man of substance.

He lived not far from the station. About ten blocks away, to the west, at the end of a dusty street which, in the afternoon light, took on a liliaceous hue, the house, with its parapet and its cornice, was set apart from the neighboring residences by a certain exotic grace, and was easy to pick out. It had a garden in the front, and an inner patio, enclosed by a wall, over the sides of which hung the limbs of a peach tree. The layout was cozy and inviting, but the grounds appeared uninhabited. In the afternoon silence, nestled among the deserted fields, this house, its aspect of a busy chalet notwithstanding, was marked by a kind of mournful tenderness, like that of a new sepulcher erected in an ancient cemetery.

When I got to the wicket, I noticed that the garden had autumn roses whose fragrance charitably alleviated the fatiguing odor of the harvest-time chaff. Between the plants the grass grew freely and so tall I could almost touch it with my hand; and an oxidized shovel leaned against the wall, with its haft half-strangled by runners of twining vines.

I unlatched the gate, crossed the garden and, not without a certain indefinable apprehension, went to knock on the front door. Minutes passed. The wind began to whistle in a crevice, aggravating the solitude of the surroundings. After a second try, I heard footsteps; soon afterwards, the door opened with a squeak of dry wood, and the master of the house appeared and greeted me.

I presented my letter. As he read, I was able to observe him at my leisure: a lofty, bald head, beard and sideburns trimmed in the manner of a clergyman's, generous lips, austere nose. It struck me that there was a touch of the mystic about him. His superciliary protuberances offset with a correct expression the impulsive tendencies of his disdainful chin. To judge from his outward aspect, this man's professional inclinations might just as soon have led him to become a missionary as a soldier. I had a desire to look at his hands to complete my impressions, but I could only see them from the back.

Folding my letter, he invited me in, and I spent the rest of the afternoon, right up until the dinner hour, getting settled. It was at the dinner table that I first noticed something odd.

As we ate I noticed that, his perfect courtesy notwithstanding, my interlocutor was bothered by something. His gaze invariably drifted towards the same corner of the room, and exhibited a vague but nagging anxiety. All I could make out near the spot where he was staring was his shadow; my furtive glances could discover nothing more. Besides, this might have been only a symptom of habitual distractedness.

I mentioned the cholera which had recently ravaged the neighboring towns. My host was a homeopath and made no secret of his satisfaction at having found in me a colleague. In light of our mutual interests, the conversation soon changed its course. The action of reduced dosages suggested to me a theory which he pressed me to explain.

"Any substance, regardless of quantity," I said, concluding my argument, "exerts an influence when brought into close proximity with Rutter's pendulum. A homeopathic globule stimulates oscillations equivalent to those produced by a dose five hundred or even a thousand times higher."

I noticed that he had gotten quite interested in my observations. The master of the house now fixed me in a stare.

"Just the same," he countered, "Reichenbach has contested this evidence. You have read your Reichenbach, I presume."

"I have read him, yes; I've attended his lectures, I've tested my radioesthetic apparatus for him, confirming Rutter's findings, and I've proven that the error lies with the German sage, not with the Englishman. The likely cause of the error is simple enough; so much so that I am surprised that it didn't occur to the illustrious discoverer of paraffin and creosote."

This drew a smile from my host; a sure sign that we understood one another.

"Did you use Rutter's prototype, or the pendulum perfected by Doctor Leger?"

"The latter," I answered.

"It's a considerably more reliable instrument," he affirmed. "And what did you conclude, according to your tests, was the cause of Reichenbach's error?"

"This: that the quantity of the substance under study has, through the power of suggestion, an effect on the influence psychics and sensitives exert over the apparatus. If the oscillation provoked by a scruple of magnesium, let us suppose, attains an amplitude of four, ideas then current about the relationship between cause and effect demanded that oscillation expand in proportion to quantity; it was thought that ten grams, for example, would drive a reading substantially higher. The Baron's sensitives were individuals unversed, for the most part, in scientific matters, but whose own practical experiences had taught them the power ideas taken for truths have over those which are purely logical or mathematical concepts. Herein then, lies the fallacy. The pendulum is unaffected by quantity; it is affected only by the nature of the substance under scrutiny; but when the sensitive believes that the larger quantity bears an influence, the effect is enhanced, since all belief is an act of will. A pendulum with which a subject interacts while ignorant of variations in quantity, confirms Rutter. The hallucination vanishes..."

"So now hallucination has come into the picture," said my interlocutor with manifest distaste.

"I am not one of those who explains away everything by ascribing it to hallucination, or who distorts or fabricates observable phenomena by filtering it through subjective states, as frequently happens. Hallucination is for me a force, more than a state of mind and, thought of in these terms, a goodly portion of phenomena can be explained. I believe that this doctrine is correct."

"Unfortunately, it's wrong. You see, I knew Holme, the medium, when I was living in London, around 1872. I later followed with vivid interest the experiments of Crookes from a radical materialist standpoint, but the evidence came home to me with the events of '74. Hallucination is not enough to explain everything. Believe me, apparitions are autonomous..."

"Permit me a slight digression," I interrupted, finding in these recollections an opportunity to corroborate my deductions about human personality. "I would like to pose a question, which I will withdraw, if you consider it indiscreet. Have you ever been a soldier?"

"For a short time; I served as a lieutenant with the army in India."

"To be sure, India must have held a wealth of curiosities for you."

"No; the war closed the road to Tibet, which is where I had wanted to go. I got as far as Cawnpore, no further. For reasons of health, I later returned to England; from England I went to Chile in 1879, and finally to this country in 1888."

"Were you ill while in India," I asked.

"Yes," he answered with the sadness of an old soldier, freshly fastening his eyes on a corner of the room.

He drooped, resting his chin on his left hand, looking right through me. His thumb began to fidget with the sparse hairs fringing the nape of his neck. I sensed that he was about to divulge some confidence to which these gestures were the prolog, and I waited. Outside, a cricket chirped in the darkness.

"I was always somewhat miserable," my host began. "This was a mystery. Soon I was forty years old and still no one knew why. What could anyone say? They hadn't understood, and thought me crazy, at the very least. I wasn't depressed; I was desperate. My wife had been dead for eight years, ignorant of the sickness devouring me, and fortunately I had no children. In you I find for the first time a man capable of understanding me."

I leaned forward appreciatively.

"Science can be so beautiful when it is uncaged, unfettered by honors and the academies! And nevertheless, you have always been sheltered by the aegis of those chiseled entablatures. Reichenbach's odylic fluids are but a prelude. The case with which you are about to become acquainted will reveal how far you have to go."

The speaker was visibly agitated. He began to jumble English phrases with slurred Castillian. His clauses took on an insistent aspect, emphatically delivered in a staccato surge of fluctuating emphases made more peculiar by a foreign accent.

"In February of 1858," he continued, "was when I lost all my happiness. You have heard of yogis, those extraordinary mendicants whose lives are divided between espionage and thaumaturgy. Travelers have popularized their exploits, which there is no need to detail. But who knows what lies at the base of their p o w e r s?"

"I believe they possess the ability to produce autosomnambulism at will, of linking themselves in some fashion with the subconscious, and becoming clairvoyant," I said.

"It's true," he blurted. "In fact, I've seen yogis perform under conditions which rule out the possibility of any fraud or chicanery. I have even photographed these sessions, and the negatives reproduced everything I had seen with my own eyes. Hallucination? Impossible! Darkroom chemicals do not hallucinate! I aspired to unravel these same powers. I had always been audacious, and had no way of knowing that I would later rue the consequences. So I set to work."

"Using what method," I queried.

Without responding, he went on: "The results were most surprising. In a short time, I began to fall asleep. At the end of two years I was able to produce conscious transport. But these practices brought me to the acme of disquiet. I felt abominably forlorn, helpless in the grip of the certain knowledge that some adverse contagion had infected my life, invading it like a venom. At the same time, I was devoured by curiosity. I was on a slippery slope, but nothing could deter me. By a sustained effort of will, I continued to keep up appearances before the world. What's more, the power awakened in me grew each day more rebellious. A prolonged displacement state preceded the crisis. I felt my personality existing outside of me. To say that my body came to be something like an affirmation of the non me, most concretely expresses this state. The impressions became more and more vivid, until they attained an excruciating lucidity and, one night, I resolved to see my double. To see what it was that had separated from me, during the ecstatic dream.

"And were you able to?"

"It was in the late afternoon, with night already coming on. The uncoupling was accomplished with the customary ease. When I recovered consciousness, there was incarnated in front of me, in a corner of the room, a form. And this form was a monkey, a horrible animal who fixed me with a gruesome stare. Since then we have never been apart. I see him constantly. I am his prisoner. Wherever he chooses, he goes, and I go with myself, with him. He is always there. He watches me constantly, but he never comes near me; he never moves, I never move…

He underscored the pronouns switched in the last phrase, to make them plainly heard. A wave of sincere concern as well as undiluted consternation swept over me. This man suffered, in fact, from an especially deleterious post-hypnotic suggestion.

"Calm yourself," I told him, feigning confidence. "Reintegration is not impossible."

"If only it were so," he bitterly replied. "But it's already too late. As you may imagine, I have lost the concept of unity. I know that two and two are four, because I have memorized it; but I no longer feel it. For me, the simplest problems of arithmetic are lifeless, because I lack the conviction of quantity. And at all times I suffer even stranger things. When I take one hand with the other, for example, I feel a thing distinctly separate from myself, as if the hand belonged to another person. At times I have double vision, because each eye acts independently of the other..."

This was, and there could be no doubt, a case of insanity of the most curious sort: one which didn't preclude the most perfect ratiocination.

"But, what about this monkey," I asked, trying to get to the bottom of the matter.

"He is as black as my own shadow, and melancholy in the way a man is. This description is exact because I am becoming this way myself. His posture is stooped, his face like the faces of all monkeys. But I sense, nonetheless, that he looks like me. Believe me, I am speaking with complete presence of mind; this animal looks like me!"

The man was, in fact, perfectly calm; and nevertheless, the idea of a simian face formed such a violent contrast with his own surpassingly refined facial angles, lofty cranium and brow, and straight, slender nose, that it strained credulity and invited attribution of its absurdity to sheer hallucination.

He tacitly noted my reaction. He rose to his feet as if he had come to a decisive resolution.

"I am going to walk around this room, so that you can see it. Observe my shadow, I implore you."

I turned up the light of the lamp, rolled the table to one end of the kitchen and began to walk around. Then the greatest possible surprise stopped me short. The shadow of this subject didn't move! Projected onto the corner at the height of the wainscot, its lower portion touching the varnished wooden floor, appeared a membrane, lengthening and shortening, according to the proximity of its owner. But there was no correlation between the image in the corner and the angle of light striking the man.

Supposing myself a victim of some grandiose temporary derangement, I determined to undeceive myself and see, by means of a decisive experiment if, indeed, the mysterious image bore any resemblance to my host. I asked him to let me capture his silhouette by passing a pencil over the profile of the shadow.

He agreed and, using four moistened bread crumbs as adhesive, I affixed a sheet of paper to the wall, in such a way that the shadow of the face stayed in the very center of the sheet. I wanted to prove, by comparing the outline of my host's profile with that of his shadow (the identical match between which would be immediately apparent, and would dispel their delusional counterpart) the origin of said shadow, whose immobility, which I intended to explain later, assured me of an exact base.

I would be lying if I said that my fingers, which otherwise drew perfectly the profile of my interlocutor, weren't trembling a little as I placed them over the shadowy stain; but I can affirm with absolute certainty that my fluttering pulse didn't ruffle what was traced. I drew the line without lifting my hand, with a blue Hardmuth pencil, and I didn't remove it from the sheet of paper until I had finished, completely convinced, by the most scrupulous observation, that the silhouette I had stenciled coincided perfectly with the outline of the shadow, and this, in turn, with the face of the deluded man.

My host followed the experiment with intense interest. When he approached me at the table, I saw his hands trembling with emotion. My heart was pounding, as if I had a presentiment of some Faustian outcome.

"Don't look," I said.

"I must see," he replied in a peremptory tone. With a shaking hand, I thrust the drawing under the light.

Both of us, recoiling, turned hideously pale. There, before our eyes, the pencil strokes had traced the outline of a hulking atavistic forehead, a flattened nose, a bestial snout. The ape! Accursed thing!

# The Miracle of Saint Wilfred

On the 15th of June, 1099, the fourth day of the third week, a twilight clouded in blood was seen for the twenty-fifth time arcing over the encampment, spreading its fan in a long train of silences above the striped tents encircling the outskirts of Jerusalem, stretching like a gory hand all the way from the gates of Damascus to where the cedar forests penetrate the Valley of Jehosophat which the Romans call the Valley of Scopus.

Over the plain which stretched between the encampment and the city, innumerable listless hulks lay scattered; cadavers remaining from the morning of the13th when the French broke through the enemy defenses and overran the fortress.

Mount Moriah loomed straight up behind the Aesterquilinine gate. To the north rose the desolate peaks of Olivet and the scandalous summit where Solomon idolatrized. Between these pinnacles sprawled the accursed valley, the valley tyrannized by the heresies of Belphegor and Moloch; where David and Jeremiah grieved and wailed; where Christ Jesus began his passion; where Joel uttered his memorable prophecy: *congregabo omnes gentes*...where Zachariah and Absalom slept; the valley where Jews from all parts of the world go to die; the valley full of shadows and tangled, black vineyards...

The walls of the city, one hundred hands high, hid from view the mountains of Judea which the Sabean king had populated with cedars. The region was sequestered, its privacy guarded by a ring of sentinels: the reddish peak of Acra, the monstrous copper cupola of the Gameat-el-Sakhra mosque raised by Omar as instructed by the patriarch Sophronius atop the Temple of Solomon, and a few scattered palms.

An agonizing thirst consumed the soldiers of the cross. The springs of Shiloh and of Rogel had been exhausted. The salty wind was blowing away from them, leaving what few clouds there were no nearer than Jericho. It was so dry, so calcinated, that even the ancient tombs seemed to clamor with thirst.

Above the tents of the besieging armies, fluttered multicolored standards among whose tatters, testaments to many trials of heroism and devotion, germinated, like future banners of glory, the thirteen crowns and the thirty-six principal crosses of heraldry, from the simple patent cross to reversed and doubly intertwined taus, which attained maximum complexity in the curious hieroglyph which served as the emblem of the Squarciaficci family.

There were Godofredo, Eustace, and Baldino; the Knights of Toulouse, of Foix, of Orange, of Rosellon, of Saint Pol, of Estoile, of Flanders, and of Normandy. They were illustrious men, one and all. Guicher had axed a lion in half; Godofredo had sliced in two a giant Saracen on the bridge to Antioch…

A plain canvas tent stood above the others. This was the tent of a lean and elderly monk who had an olive staff, and lived out his days with the entire length of his beard soaked in tears. This was Peter the Hermit.

This monk knew that the noble city founded in the 2023rd year of the world was, like so many who had lived within its precincts, a martyr.

From the sons of Jeb up through Seth, from Jonah through Manasses, through Nebuchadnezzar, through Ptolemy the Younger, through the two Antiochuses, the Great and the Epiphanous, through Pompey, through Crassus, through Antigone, through Herod, through Titus, through Hadrian, through Cosroes, through Omar - what blood had spattered its foundation stones, what desolation had fallen over the queen glorified by Tobias' salutation: *Jerusalem, civitas Dei, luce splendida fulgebis!* Like Saint Jerome, Peter observed that in this city there was not a single bird to be seen.

✳✳✳

That afternoon, a communiqué dispatched from Kaloni informed Godofredo that in the port of Jaffa there sat at anchor various Pisan and Genoan ships in which had come sailors waiting to build machines of war designed by Raymond of Foix.

The sun had gone down when four knights, envoyed to Jaffa to guard the newly moored ships, set out along the road from Arimathaea. They were Raimundo Pileto, Acardo of Mommellou, Guillermo of Sabran and Wilfred of Hohenstein, whom they called the Knight of the White Helmet.

He was blond and strong as an archangel. On his German shield which, as was the custom of the time, bore no motto, there was emblazoned a lily stamped in tin and set against a green field. This lily, shaped like a halberd, was, of all heraldic flowers, the only one shown in open bloom; this was because those in France stayed perpetually in bud.

But the extraordinary thing about the knight's armor was his helmet of whitish metal, whose splendor stood out from the rest because of the crest which the helmets of the other crusaders lacked. The noseplate of this helmet, exaggeratedly dividing the space between his brows and sloping between his eyes like a beak, gave his face the expression of a gyrfalcon.

Recounted about this ornament is an odd legend. It is said that he married his lady when he was twenty years old, and killed her a year later in a fit of jealous rage. When the innocence of his victim was afterwards discovered, the Lord of Hohenstein sued for pardon from Peter the Hermit, who commended him to serve in the Holy Wars as a soldier of Christ, and hung on his chest the pilgrims' cross.

Before he left, the young man went to pray at the tomb of his wife. On this sepulcher had grown a lily which he decided to pick and carry with him as a memento; it is said that when he snipped it, the flower was transformed into a silvery white helmet, which is how he got his distinctive name. It was rumored that he had caused the miracle of making lilies shower over the resting place of his beloved, and the hero's comrades had no reason to doubt the veracity of this tale, especially as he had acquitted himself with valor and strictly kept his vow of chastity.

Night was already dense over the mountains. The knights crossed them at a trot in their clattering cavalcade, like four shadows borne on a whisper of steel; they crossed the sterile strip which united Jerusalem with Sikem and Neapolis; they crossed the torrent where David gathered five stones to do battle with the giant; they crossed the valley of Terebinth, and that of Jeremiah, descending from the torturous Judean cliffs populated by wild boar; they passed the suburbs of Arimathaea, and those of Lydia, dotted with the date palms under the shade of which Peter cured the paralytic; they came to the Well of the Virgin, on the Plain of Sharon, with its tulips and gillyflowers outspread before them from Gaza to Carmel, and from the mountains of Judea to those of Samaria, which betrayed themselves in the darkness with the aroma of their blossoms. Scene after scene from holy scripture was called forth by the places the valiant warriors now transited.

Wilfred had ridden ahead a bit. The other three kept their pious conversation, and the Lord of Sabran related to his companions the history of the city for which they were headed.

Jaffa was, he said, of the lineage of Dan and more ancient than the flood. Noah died there; to it floated the barges of Hiram laden with cedars; from it Jonas embarked to cross the sea, those Great Waters which "saw God and were afraid," as the Psalms say; it suffered the weight of five invasions and was put to the torch by Judas Macabee. There Peter resurrected Tabitha; there Cestius and Vespasian replenished their legions with gold; and now, in its citadel, commanding in the name of the Sultan, was the ferocious Abu Djezzar Mohamed Ibn El Thayyib El Achary, who was familiarly called Abu Djezzar, and whose mercenaries patrolled the parapets, running their eyes over the surrounding landscape, searching for signs of the soldiers of Christ.

The Lord of Mommellou added in his turn that Jaffa had figured in pagan myth. It was named after one of the daughters of Aeolus, and Saint Jerome recounts that it was the site of the boulder to which Andromeda was chained for Neptune's monster. Pliny adds that Escaurus brought to Rome the bones of said animal; and Pausanias that there has existed all along at Jaffa the fountain where Perseus cleansed his hands of the soil of combat.

All this was told by the Knights Acardo of Mommellou and Guillermo of Sabran, because they were learned in history which they had absorbed from the parchments of the monasteries.

Suddenly, as their little band arrived at the ruins of a dry cistern, it became clear that Wilfred was no longer with them. Unquestionably he had wandered into dangerous territory; but they couldn't stop to look for him, because the fate of the holy city depended on the ships they were going to guard. And though there was no time to spare, they galloped here and there, blowing their horns at the nearby walls.

✳✳✳

Abu Djezzar governed the citadel. The fortress rose vertically, dominating the sea, between groves of fig and pomegranate trees. A thousand Moslems defended themselves there, waiting for reinforcements from Caesarea or from Solimah. The fosses were full of water and they had shut the portcullises, leaving little sanctuary for roving marauders.

Wilfred of Hohenstein, stripped of his arms, was dragged before the lord of the citadel. He was a Moslem with aquiline eyes and a profile as sharp as a hatchet.

"Dog," he spat, barely shooting him a glance; "we know that your soldiers are dying of thirst beneath the walls of Solimah. Tell me, if you know, why the Christians hold out any hope."

A heroic smile lit the young knight's face.

"Saracen," he replied, "the Earls of Flanders and of Normandy are camped to the north, in the spot where Saint Stephen was stoned; Godofredo and Tancred are deployed in the west; the Earl of Saint-Gilles to the south, on Mount Zion. You know where our troops are positioned, and also that the soldiers of Christ never retreat. Well, then, know this, Saracen: before the month is out, the soldiers of Christ will enter Jerusalem from the north, the west, and the south."

Abu Djezzar reddened with rage.

"Cut some planks," he screamed to his soldiers, "make a cross and nail this dog to it. Let him die like his god!"

Three hours later, the soldiers came in groups to contemplate the martyr. Wilfred of Hohenstein, nailed to a very short cross, seemed dead where he hung. Entirely naked, red streaks crisscrossing his body, his head bent, his blond hair covering his eyes, his hands and feet swathed in purple, he looked like an altarpiece effigy. Death did not tarnish his youth, but aggrandized it even more like a fine glaze on a marble statue. Above the ruined city, forsaken under the angry sky, the scaffold overlooked the sea. And the soldiers admired, in hushed voices, with words barbarously phrased in guttural ejaculations, this young enemy, so virile beneath the blond hair already girded by a halo of apotheosis.

The body of Wilfred of Hohenstein was not without a certain grace. It was very pale, almost transparent, like an alabaster vase which has spilled all its wine; and under his half-open eyelids, glimmered two faint blue stars.

A Syrian vulture, at an immense altitude, jostled itself among the stratospheric slendors. The soldiers saw it and then they remembered. Although the agony of the knight had been prolonged, there could be no doubt that he was dead. The aga walked over to him and lifted one of his eyelids. The little blue star had been extinguished at the bottom of its orbit. From the labial commissure, trickled a thread of blood...

No one dared to slap his face, despite that being the custom, because his dreaming pacified with its immense whiteness. They simply held the cross and began to pry him loose. But his right hand resisted somewhat, so the aga chopped it off with his scimitar, leaving it nailed to the timber and, so that this artifact could serve as a warning to other dogs, resolved to keep it in the armory.

The hand remained there for a month. No one even remembered it when, on the 12th of July, 1099, a Saracen emissary rode in on his moribund horse to tell Abu Djezzar that the Christians, propping scaling ladders against the walls of Solimah as dawn broke, and enclosed in ingenious wooden fortresses, had rained over the Prophet's faithful a deluge of boiling oil and pitch.

Abu Djezzar ordered swords to be sharpened and descended to the armory to inspect the accouterments of his knights and pawns. The weapons gleamed in the half-light of the hall. There were cuirasses from Egypt, yataghans from Damascus, Spanish lances more than ten hands long; oval shields made from hippopotamus hide, captured Nubian stirrups trimmed for use by Berbers and Byzantine daggers which flowed like water.

The Moslem ran a satisfied eye over this arsenal, consolidated by the Caliph from caches culled from far and wide. The patter of his slippers resounded in the vaults of the gallery and, superbly draped in his elegant burnoose, he examined the munitions thoroughly.

In the intense summer heat, he had taken off his turban and on the occiput of his shaved head showed the tuft of hair by which the angel Gabriel would conduct him to Paradise on the Day of Judgment. There swam in his eyes two nervous sparks and, beneath his twitching lip, his teeth were clenched with a sinister shine.

From where he stood he could dimly descry, concealed in the shadows, the cross where the hand of the martyr was yellowing. And, as his gaze shifted to one of the racks in the armory, he backed closer, closer, until he was standing directly underneath it.

At this moment it was three in the afternoon. The Knight of Estoile was breaching the battlements of Jerusalem.

As the aga appeared in the doorway to announce what had happened, Abu Djezzar exploded, screaming, "May Allah exterminate them all! Accursed dogs!"

He wasn't able to finish. The hand sprang to life, coiled like a claw, wriggled on its spike, and snatched the infidel's topknot between its fingers.

The aga, crazed with horror, fled to the roof of the citadel. The soldiers scurried below to help, but none dared touch the formidable relic that invincibly kept the captured enemy in its grip.

Abu Djezzar already lay dead at the foot of the cross, his tongue lolling between his teeth, his arms akimbo from convulsing.

That same afternoon, the aga ordered the sinister crucifix to be hurled from the battlements, and never since has the hand unclenched. And the Christians of Jaffa, learning of the incident from a prisoner of the citadel taken a few days later, carried this trophy in a public procession, and erected a shrine to the Knight of the White Helmet who suffered death on the cross at the hands of the infidels the 12th of July in the year of our Lord 1099.

✳✳✳

Today, in the Franciscan monastery at Jaffa, under a crystal dome, nailed to a slab of wood, and clutching a fistful of still-fresh hair, as if it were a gift of consolation for the seventeenth agony of Jerusalem, can be seen the white hand of Saint Wilfred of Hohenstein.

# The Bloat - Toad

One day, long ago, playing in the courtyard of the house where my family lived, I noticed that a little toad, instead of fleeing like his more corpulent fellows, had inflated himself extraordinarily under the hailstorm of rocks I rained on him. Toads horrified me and one of my pastimes was to flatten as many as I could. Thus it wasn't long before the diminutive and obstinate amphibian succumbed to the blows of my stones. Like all boys raised in the semirural surroundings of our provincial cities, I was an expert about lizards and toads. What's more, our house was situated near a gully which cut across the city, contributing to the frequency of my relations with such vermin. I go into these details so that it will be well understood how surprised I was to note that the atrabilious toadlet was of a variety entirely unfamiliar to me. This circumstance called for consultation, so I scooped up my victim with all appropriate precaution, and went to ask the advice of the old creature who lived on the hill, confident of my worth as a hunter and trapper. I was eight years old and she was seventy. The subject was of interest to us both. The good woman was, as usual, stationed in the kitchen doorway, and I waited to be admitted with the customary benevolence before I made my report, but I had barely begun when she suddenly jumped up, rushed towards me, and snatched the mangled little animal from my hands.

"Thank God you didn't keep it," she exclaimed with gestures of the profoundest relief. "It must be incinerated," she said.

"Incinerated," I asked, but what did it matter if it was already dead?

"Don't you know that this is a bloat toad," my interlocutor prodded in a mysterious tone, "and that this animal will come back to life if it isn't burned? Who told you to kill it? This is what comes of your rock-throwing! Now I'm going to tell you what happened to my friend Antonia, may she rest in peace."

As she spoke, I gathered and ignited some wood chips atop which I laid the cadaver of the toad.

"A bloat-toad," I blurted, my appalled delinquent boy's skin crawling with terror. "A bloat-toad!" And I shook my fingers as if the toad's sticky coldness had glued them together. "A toad come alive again!" It was enough to freeze the brain of the toughest of men.

"Did you think you were going to have a new batrachiomachia on your hands," Julia here interrupted with all the amiable ease of her thirty year old's coquetry.

"Not at all, Señorita," replied the old woman. "But it's a story that is best left untold."

Julia smiled. "Can you imagine, then, how much I would like to hear it?"

"I'll be glad to tell you - all the more so since I'll have the pleasure of dispelling your doubting smile."

And as my fateful hunting trophy burned to a crisp, the old creature stitched a narrative which ran as follows:

Antonia, her friend, a soldier's widow, lived with the only son she had had with him, in a very poor little house distant from any town. The boy labored for them both, chopping wood from the neighboring forest, and thus they passed year after year, making life's journey on tiptoe. One afternoon, as was his custom, he returned to take his coffee, happy, healthy, vigorous, with his axe slung over his shoulder. And as he sat, he told his mother how, among the tangled roots of a certain old tree he had come upon a bloat-toad, to whose swellings and puffings he paid no attention, regarding them as scant protection against being squashed like a pancake under the blade of his axe.

On hearing this, the poor old lady was fraught with affliction, pleading with him to take her to the murder site to burn the cadaver of the animal.

"I hope you know," she said to him, "that the bloat-toad never forgives those who offend it. If you don't burn it, it will revive, follow the trail of its killer, and it won't rest until it can mete the same fate to that guilty party."

The cheerful boy laughed grandly at the tale, trying to convince the poor old woman that such stories were humbug, silly hoaxes designed to frighten mischievous children, and was indignant to find her placing credence in such yarns. She insisted, nevertheless, on accompanying him to burn the remains of the animal. All levity was useless. She prattled on about directions and distance to the site, on the damage that could be caused, and about how old she was feeling amidst the serenity of the November afternoon. At all costs she wanted to go and he decided to go along with her.

It wasn't very far; a few hundred yards at the most. They could easily get there by way of the trunk of a recently felled tree, but though they squeezed through the tangled thickets and clambered among the reeds and the overhanging branches, and poked among the leaves and broken twigs with a stick, the corpse of the bloat-toad was nowhere to be seen.

"Didn't I tell you," she exclaimed, bursting into tears. "You see what has happened? Now there is no remedy for the situation. May Saint Anthony protect you!"

"But it's nonsense to upset yourself this way. The toad has been carried away by ants or eaten by some hungry skunk. What carrying on, crying over a toad! Anyway, we'd better head home. It's already getting dark, and you know how slippery the meadows can be when they're wet."

They wound their way back to the little house, she crying all the while, he trying to distract her with chat about the cornfields that promised a good crop if rain came, even resorting to jokes and gibes in the face of her stubborn distress. It was almost dark when they got home. After a meticulous inspection of all the nooks and crannies, which drew the boy's laughter all over again, they ate, in silence, on the patio, by the light of the swollen moon, and he had already slumped onto his bunk when Antonia declared that she intended to enclose herself, from that night forward, in an old wooden storage chest she kept, so that she could sleep inside of it.

Over his protests, she pleaded with him to do the same. He had no doubt that she was going senile, the poor thing. Who would dream of sleeping with such heat, he mulled, inside a box that surely would be full of disgusting bugs!

But such were the supplications of the old woman that the boy, seeing the devoutness of her desire, agreed to humor her caprice. The chest was large and, though somewhat dilapidated, not altogether awful. With great solicitude, a bed was arrayed in the bottom, the sad widow placed herself inside and, seated within this protective cradle, resigned herself to spending a wakeless night, ready to slam shut the lid at the first sign of danger.

From the moon, slung low in the sky and bathing the room with its silver light, she calculated that it must be about midnight when, suddenly, a black lump, almost imperceptible, leapt over the sill of the door, which had been left open on account of the stifling heat. Antonia was paralyzed with fear.

The vengeful animal, squatting on its haunches, just sat there, as if meditating on a plan. What evil the boy had done by laughing! This lugubrious little figure, motionless in the doorway flooded by moonlight, inflated itself extraordinarily, assuming monstrous proportions. But wasn't it just one of the same familiar toads which came around the house every evening in search of insects? She drew a quick breath, sustained by this idea. Abruptly, wildly, the bloat-toad made a sudden leap, then another, in the direction of the chest. His intention was plain. He didn't hurry, as if he were sure of his prize. With an expression of unspeakable horror, Antonia turned to look at her son; he was sleeping, wrapped in dreams, breathing slowly and monotonously.

Then, frantically, but without making a noise, she drew shut the lid of the heavy wooden chest with a fumbling hand. The animal didn't stop. It continued to hop. It was already at the foot of the chest. It turned around, circled slowly, deliberately, paused at one of the corners and, all at once, with a leap incredible for its tiny size, planted itself on the lid.

Antonia didn't dare make the slightest move. Her entire being was concentrated in her eyes. Moonlight immersed the entire room now. And here's what happened next: the toad began to inflate, to swell, to puff up by degrees, bulging, expanding, ballooning in a prodigious fashion, until it had tripled in size. It stayed that way for at least a minute, during which the poor woman felt pass through her heart all the torments of the damned. Then it began to reduce itself and reduce itself until it reassumed its original form, hopped to the ground, headed for the door, and crossed the patio, finally losing itself amongst the shrubbery.

It was only then that Antonia, trembling from head to foot, summoned the strength to venture out of the chest. Inch by inch, with abrupt little thrusts, she levered the lid. What met her eyes was so horrible that she died a few months later from the fright it produced.

With mortal coldness she exited the open chest, and found the boy already frozen and rigid beneath the sad light. The corpse-enshrouding moon had wreathed its sepulchral plunder, already turned to stone, with an inexplicable bath of frost.

# Metamusic

*A*s it had been several weeks since I'd seen him, when I bumped into him I asked, "Have you been ill?"

"No, I've never felt better and I'm merry as a cricket. If you only knew what I've absorbed during two months of seclusion!"

It had been, in fact, two months, during which time he had absented himself from the meetings of his literary club, his favorite cafes, and even from his chosen paradise, the Opera, for which he had a special fondness.

Poor John had a weakness: music. In good times, when his properous and respected father secured perennial box seats, John could abandon himself to his passion in sumptuous comfort. Then came the downfall: demotion, foreclosed mortgages, the closing of accounts...the old man died from despair and John found himself alone in that singular state of autonomy known as orphanhood, which exiled him first to a country cottage, then to a boarding house that served two meals a day, without wine.

So as not to end up a guest at the jail, he took employment doing jobs which demanded more and more and paid less and less; but there are timid beings who, even in their prime, fear life enough to respect it, and would rather settle for handouts than dream of taking risks.

Juan's existence turned thoroughly monotonous. His office, his books, and his booth in paradise became a burden to him and a pointless luxury. He studied a great deal, molding himself into a formidable theorist. Similarities of condition and opinion drew us together, nurtured our friendship, and ultimately united us in sincere affection. The only thing which separated us was music. I never understood a word of his dissertations about the subject, and could never get worked up over them or get into their spirit; it all seemed a useless exercise to me, inasmuch as there was no point in creating an "art" out of something defiant towards reason and as, in art, comprehension was intimately tied to felt emotion, and I felt nothing about music, it was clear that I didn't understand it.

This nearly made my friend despondent, and his eloquence grew in proportion to my incapacity to enjoy what was, for him, a panoply of superior emotion, but which was, for me, only so much gabble and confusion.

He continued to hone his expertise at the piano, a magnificent instrument whose chords only reinforced his sensibilities, while my rebellious emotions refused to be won over one iota.

"Words cannot express it," he said, "but listen; open wide the doors of your spirit; it's impossible that you can fail to understand."

And his fingers ran up and down the keyboard with a kind of mystic exhilaration.

And so our discussions ran every Saturday evening, alternating between lyrical dissertations with scientific themes in which John was very forceful, and recited verse. At three the following morning was the hour we customarily broke off. So much the more, then, would our conversation be prolonged, after eight weeks of separation.

"And how is your music coming along, John?"

"I'll show you. I've made some important discoveries."

His physiognomy took on a serious character, which I believed was put on for dramatic effect. But it occurred to me to ask, "Have you been composing?"

His eyes gleamed.

"Much better than that. You are a soulmate so I know I can tell you. It's Saturday night, of course; we're at home; but you must tell no one, eh? No one," he added in an almost forbidding tone.

He was quiet a moment; then he tugged at my ear confidentially, as a malicious smile played over his feverish lips.

"You're going to understand at last, you'll see. Until next Saturday, then…?"

And as he stood there, staring at me inquisitively, he added, as I bolted from his stoop to chase after a streetcar, but in such a way that only I could hear him, "The colors of music!"

It was Wednesday. It was necessary for me to wait three days to learn the meaning of that phrase. "The colors of music," he had said. Was he referring to some kind of modality for hearing colors? Impossible! John is too level-headed to fall for anything of that sort. He seemed excited, but nothing indicated a derangement of his faculties. After all, why couldn't there be some truth to his discovery? He knows a lot, he's ingenious, persevering, thorough…Music was based on a foundation of mathematics, after all, and mathematics was the salt of the spirit. All I could do was wait and give the matter time.

But, my resignation notwithstanding, an intense curiosity got the better of me; and a hypocritically ingenuous pretext for breaking the deadlock was not slow in presenting itself.

John was ill, there could be no doubt, I told myself. To abandon him in such a situation would be inexcusable. The best thing would be to see him, talk things over, make the best of a bad situation, and do whatever could be done to prevent matters from becoming worse. I decided to go see him. That same night I went and, I must admit, in retrospect, that my visit was made more out of curiosity than concern.

It was nine o'clock by the time I got to his house. The door was closed. An unknown servant came to open it. I thought it best to present myself as a trusted friend and, after exchanging greetings, I asked in my most confidential tone:

"Is John in?"

"No, sir. He has gone out."

"Do you expect him to return soon?"

"He didn't say."

"If he'll be coming back soon," I added insistently, "I'll wait for him in his room, if you don't mind. I am a close friend and have something urgent to discuss with him."

"Sometimes he doesn't come home all night."

This evasion revealed that he was merely doing as he'd been instructed, and I decided to withdraw without pressing the matter. I went again Thursday and Friday, with the same result. John didn't want to receive me; and this, frankly, exasperated me. Saturday I mustered all my strength to master my curiosity; I wouldn't go. But come Saturday evening at nine o'clock this puerile conceit had crumbled. John himself opened the door.

"You must forgive me; I know you've been looking for me; I wasn't here; I had to go out every night."

"Yes, you've become a mysterious personage."

"I take it you're interested in seeing my invention."

"To see it, not much; but, frankly, to hear you speak of the colors of music, you gave me some cause for concern."

"I'm sorry, my friend. But, really, there's no need to worry on my account. I want you to believe what I've been telling you, and I hasten to assure you that I am not mad. Your doubt wounds my inventor's pride, but we are such good friends I promise I won't wreak vengeance."

Meanwhile, we had crossed a patio full of plants. We entered a hallway, doubled back to the right, and John opened a door, saying, "Go on in, I'll have some coffee made for us."

It was his room, as I had seen it so many times: with his desk, his wardrobe closet, his bookcase, his wrought iron bedstead. I noted that the piano was missing. At this moment, John came back.

"What happened to the piano?"

"It's in the adjoining suite. I am rich now. I have two salons."

"Such opulence!"

And this led us to the subject at hand.

John, who sipped his coffee with delight, began calmly, "Let's talk seriously. You are going to see something interesting. You are going to see, mark me well. This has nothing to do with theory. Every musical note possesses its own color, and this isn't arbitrary, but real. Hallucinations and whatever other craziness you may imagine have nothing to do with what you are about to see. Machines don't lie, and my apparatus makes the colors of music perceptible. Three years before we met, I undertook the experiments which have now been crowned with success. No one in the house knew what I was up to; even though there was no privacy in the place, as you will recall. The house of a widower with grown sons...I bring this up in order to excuse my secrecy, which I hope you won't attribute to mistrust; it's just that I wanted to give you a bit of background, before beginning our little scientific jaunt."

We lit cigarettes, and John continued, "We know from the unified field theory that motion is, according to the case, light, heat, sound, and so on, depending on the differences - which essentially don't exist, but are only the modes of perception of our nervous system - in the number of vibrations of the etheric wave.

Thus it is then, that in all sound there is light, heat, and latent electricity, just as in all light there is electricity, heat, and sound. The ultraviolet of the spectrum signals the limit at which light is already heat, and at which heat, when it reaches a certain temperature, is converted into light...and this applies to electricity, as well. Why shouldn't it be the same case with sound,' I asked; and since that moment I have stuck to my problem.

The musical scale is represented by a series of numbers whose proportional interrelationship, starting with do as the primary unit, is well known; harmony is constituted by the interactions of numerical proportions or, stated another way, comprised of the relationships of aerial vibrations accompanying an accord of dissimilar movements.

In all music, the same thing happens, whatever may have been its historical sequence of development. The Greeks, who knew nothing but three of the consonances of the scale, arrived at identical proportions: 1 to 2, 3 to 2, 4 to 3. This, as you will observe, is mathematical. Among light waves an equal relationship must obtain, and this comparison is not new. The 1 of do is represented by vibrations of 369 millionths of a millimeter which engenders violet, and the 2 of the octave is represented by double that amount, or the 738 which produce red. Each of the rest of the notes similarly corresponds to one color.

Next, my thinking proceeded as follows:

When we hear a sound, we don't see light, we don't feel heat, we don't sense the electricity which is produced, because calorific, luminous, and electrical waves are imperceptible at their own amplitude. By the same token, we cannot hear light sing, although light really and truly does sing, when its vibrations, which constitute colors, form harmonic proportions. Every sensory perception has a limit of intensity, beyond which it passes into imperceptibility by us. These limits do not coincide, in the majority of cases, but are filtered through a whole range of differentiation effected by the senses in superior organisms, and this is why, when a vibration is initiated, we cannot perceive more than one of the movements engendered, because the wavelength of the others has exceeded the threshold of human perception. At times, however, two or more sensory impressions are engendered by the same stimulus. Thus, we see the color of a light, we feel its heat, and we sense its electricity…"

All this was logical; but where sound was concerned, I had a very basic objection to make and I made it: "What you've been saying is clear enough, but your principle doesn't apply to sound, because sound is an aerial vibration, while the others are etheric vibrations."

"Indeed," he retorted, "but the aerial wave, having propagated itself, provokes etheric waves, when the ether between the molecules of air is displaced. What is this second vibration? I have been able to demonstrate that it is light. Who knows if tomorrow an ultrasensitive thermometer will not determine the temperature of sound?

An insightful man unjustifiably forgotten, Louis Lucas, said that which I am going to read to you from his *New Chemistry*: 'If one studies with care the properties of the monochord, one will note that in all sonic hierarchies, there exist no more than three points of primary importance: the keynote, the fifth and the third, the octave being a reproduction of them at various heights, preserving the three resonances with the keynote acting as a fulcrum; the fifth is its antagonist and the third an indifferent bystander, ready to follow whichever of the two contraries attains superiority.

This is the same relationship we find in three simple substances, whose relative importance there is no need to record: hydrogen, nitrogen, and oxygen. The first, by its absolute negativism in the presence of other metalloids, by its essentially irreducible properties, takes the place of the keynote or relative rest; oxygen, by virtue of its antagonistic properties, occupies the place of the fifth; and finally nitrogen, whose indifference is well known, is assigned the position of the third.'

From this, you will see that I am not alone in my conjectures, and that it doesn't follow that I am going too far; moreover, you will see just how careful I have been when we repeat the experiment.

Before doing anything else, I was confronted by three choices: either to filter sound through a body which would absorb it, letting nothing pass through except light waves, using something resembling animal carbon for chemical colorants; to construct chords so powerful that their vibrations could be counted not by thousandths but by millionths and billionths to the second, in order to transform my music into light; or to reduce the expansion of the light wave, invisible in sound, by containing its release, reflecting it, and amplifying it until it broke through the threshold of perception, and appeared on a conveniently arranged screen. Of the three possible methods, I chose the last; the first two would have required extensive new development, while the third merely calls for a variant of existing equipment.

"Age dum," he proceeded, evoking his Latin, while opening the door to an adjoining room. "Here you have my apparatus." He was pointing to a trestle on top of which rested a box about two meters wide, resembling a coffin. At one end, it was surmounted by a parabolic tent made from a sort of cambric. On the lid, near the other end, jutted a crystal strip which reminded me of a facet of a prism. A white screen crested the mysterious casket, projecting from a metal support mounted at the midpoint of the lid.

John poised himself above the apparatus and I was seated on the piano bench.

"Listen attentively."

"I'm all yours."

"The tent which you see here collects sound waves. It is attached to the bottom of a tube of double-thick black glass, in which the vacuum is raised to a millionth atmosphere. The double-thick tube is designed to hold a layer of water. Sound dies in it and in the dense cushion which surrounds it. This isolates the light wave whose expansion must be arrested so that the suprasensible amplitude cannot overtake it. The black glass does the trick and, aided by the refraction of the water, brings about almost total reduction. What's more the water serves to absorb the resulting heat."

"And why the black glass?"

"Because the vibration of black light is superior to all others; consequently, the space between vibratory impulses is restricted and, since the rest cannot pass through the interstices, they reflect one another. This is analogous to a trough filled with spinning tops which dance while keeping their respective distances proportionate to size. A large top, though moving at minor velocity, tries to pass; but this produces a collision which obliges it to turn back."

"And the others - don't they also retrocede?"

"This is the circumstance which the water is charged with preventing."

"Alright. Go on."

"The shortened light wave finds itself at the end of the tube with a disk of mercury blocking its path."

"Ah, the inevitable mercury."

"Yes, mercury. When Professor Lippmann employed it to correct the interference of light waves in his work on color photography, I benefitted from the data; and the result has not disappointed my expectations. Accordingly, my mercury disk, mounted at an angle in the barrel of the tube, restrains the wave passing through the tube, and bends it upwards, channeling it into a second tube. In this second tube, there are deployed three *unbreakable* prisms, which amplify the light wave until it reaches the point at which it can be perceived as an optical sensation. The number of prisms is determined by trial and error, using only the naked eye, and the last of them, sealing the end of the tube, is that which you see protruding here. We have, then, suppressed sonic vibration, reduced the amplitude of the light wave, contained its advance and reinforced its action. That leaves nothing but seeing it."

"And can it be seen?"

"I can see it at will; I see it on this screen; but one thing is missing. This thing is my piano, whose keyboard must be transformed into a series of seven white and seven black keys, to maintain the true relationship of the transpositions of one tonic note to another; a relationship which establishes itself by multiplying the note by the interval of the minor semitone.

Thus converted, my piano becomes a precision instrument, although much more difficult to master. Ordinary pianos, built on the principle of the tempered scale, which I will get back to later, muffle the difference between tones and major and minor semitones, so that all the sounds of the octave are reduced by twelve, when there are fourteen in reality. My modified keyboard, on the other hand, is precise and comprehensive.

The adoption of this reform is equivalent to abolishing with one stroke the tempered scale in current use, along with what, in all fairness, must be conceded are the enormous strides made by instrumental music since the era of Sebastian Bach, who penned no fewer than forty-eight compositions. Are you following me, so far?"

"What do I know about any of this? All I can see is that you have chosen me the way one chooses a wall to bounce a ball against."

"I suppose it's useless to remind you that nothing can stand up without having something else opposing it."

We both shut up, smiling. Then John resumed, "At least you understand, then, that music expresses nothing?"

"In the face of this odd question which abruptly re-routed the course of our discussion, I asked in turn, "Have you read Hanslick?"

"Yes, why?"

"Because Hanslick, whose critical competence I wouldn't dare dispute, maintains that music expresses nothing, that it only evokes sentiments."

"Did Hanslick say that? Well then, without being a German critic, I concur; though, at the same time, I contend that music is the mathematical expression of the soul."

"Words…"

"No. Perfectly demonstrable facts. If you multiply the semidiameter of the world by 36, you obtain the five musical scales of Plato, which correspond to the five senses."

"And why 36?"

"There are two reasons: the first is mathematics, and the other is physics. According to the first, 36 numbers are needed to fill the intervals of the octaves, the fourths and the fifths up to 27, with harmonic numbers."

"And why 27?"

"Because 27 is the sum of the cubed numbers 1 and 8; of the lineals 2 and 3; and of the planars 4 and 9; which is to say, of the mathematical bases of the universe. The psychic reason consists in that this number 36, the total of the harmonic numbers, represents that of the human emotions."

"What!"

"The Venetian Gozzi, as well as Goethe and Schiller, affirm that there cannot exist but 36 dramatic emotions. One scholar, J. Polti, demonstrated, in the year 1894, if I am not mistaken, that the quantity is exact and that the number of human emotions doesn't exceed 36."

"How curious!"

"Indeed; and more curious still if you take into account my own observations. The sum or absolute value of the ciphers of 36 is 9, an irreducible number; all the multiples repeat it if they themselves are subordinated to the same equation. The 1 and the 9 are the only absolute or permanent numbers; hence, 27 and 36, having 9 as the absolute value of their ciphers, are numbers of the same category. This creates, what is more, a proportion. 27, being the total of the geometric bases, is to 36, the total of the human emotions, as X, the soul, is to the absolute 9. Putting the equation into practice will confirm that the unknown term is 6. Six, fix this well: the double measure which in the sacred symbology of the ancients signified the equilibrium of the universe. Do you follow me?"

His expression had become luminous and strange.

"The universe is music," he continued animatedly. Pythagoras was right, and from Timaeus through Kepler, all the thinkers have spoken of this harmony. Erastosthenes came to determine the celestial scale, the tones and semitones quavering between the stars. I believe I have found something better: the lost notes of the music of the spheres, with which I can reproduce, in geometrically combined colors, the scheme of the Cosmos…"

What was he saying with this hallucination? What turbillion of extravagances was whirling in his head?…Almost before I had time to notice it, the piano began to play.

John returned to being the inspired player of former days, as his fingers caressed the keys.

"My music," he was saying, "is formed by chords in third minor introduced in the seventeenth century, which Mozart himself considered imperfect, despite the facts to the contrary; but his recourse consisted of adopting those same inverse chords which earned the music of Palestrina the title of 'angelic melodies'…"

In truth, even my refractory nature was moved by those sounds. They had nothing in common with normal harmonies, though it might be said they weren't even music in the traditional sense; what's certain is that they immersed the spirit in a serene ecstasy, like something spoken in antiquity and heard at a great distance.

John continued:

"Observe on the screen the distribution of colors which accompanies the musical emission. That which you are hearing is a harmony in which specific notes enter from each planet in the solar system; and this simple conjunction terminates with the sublime octave of the sun, which I have never been so insolent as to invoke, being afraid to produce excessively powerful influences.Don't you feel something strange?"

I felt, in fact, as if the atmosphere of the room were stirred by invisible presences. Deafening gusts thundered through its ambit. And intersecting the beatitude with which the solemn sweetness of this harmony regaled me, was a kind of electric aura which threatened to freeze me with fright. But I couldn't distinguish anything on the screen but a vague phosphorescence and something like sketchy figures…

Suddenly I understood. In our shared exaltation, we had forgotten to switch off the flow of light.

I went to do it, when John screamed violently, in the midst of a stupendous sound produced by the instrument, "Look now!"

I too, let out a scream, then something horrific happened.

A dazzling, flaring flame erupted from the center of the screen. John, his hair standing on end, jumped to his feet, in utter panic. His eyes began to fizzle, pop, and evaporate like two drops of water beneath which a flame has been lit and he, insensitive to pain, radiant with madness, exclaimed, as he grasped me by the arms:

"The octave of the sun, old chap, the octave of the sun!"

sions about his favorite subject were endless. My friend was inspired when speaking of it, with a quiet ardor which belied his enthusiasm and became translucent in the brilliance of his eyes.

Whenever I saw him, he would be pacing in his room, intensely holding forth, with his face almost jutting into mine, his nose and chin pale and beardless, his eyes stricken with a peculiar glaze, his hands callused from labor and from handling chemicals all the time.

He prowled from the door to the window sill and back again, only repeating that he would soon harness an unknown force of awesome power. The unveiling of such extraphysical forces would alter the most rigid laws of science, he said, while concomitantly affirming the teachings of occult arcana, which would enlarge human knowledge a hundredfold.

"The identification of the mind with the directive forces of the universe, he would often end by volunteering, philosophically, "becomes clearer and clearer; and the day is coming when we will know what regulates them without benefit of intermediary machinery, which in reality is nothing but a hindrance. Machines must be considered as appendages with which human beings complete themselves, by activating potentials already latent in themselves, which is proven by their ability to conceive and execute such mechanical adjuncts in the first place; adjuncts, which, after all, are elaborations, of varying complexity, of the simple pole which extends the arm to help snatch a peach. Think of the power of the human mind, all by itself! The memory can suppress two fundamental concepts, which are both fundamental realities and fundamental obstacles - space and time - to instantaneously evoke a place seen ten years ago and a thousand leagues away; not to mention certain cases of telepathic bilocation, which illustrate this theory even better. In as much as this is true, it is an illustration of the imperative driving the human race to strive to abolish everything intermediate between the mind and the transcendent vital forces of the universe, by suppressing material intrusions as much as possible, another axiom of occult philosophy. There are steps and procedures which can be adopted to place the organism under a set of special conditions favorable to stimulating the mind in such a way as to accustom it to direct communication with the aforementioned forces. Take the case of magic. It is a case which only myopics fail to perceive in all its simple luminosity. We have been speaking of memory. Calculus also demonstrates a direct relationship; if calculus enables us to determine the position of an unknown star in a point in space, it's because there are parallels between the laws which rule human thought and those which govern the universe. This principle is illustrated everywhere: it is the determination of material facts by means of mental laws. The star has to be there, because our mathematical reason has determined it to be so, and this sanction is almost equivalent to creating it."

I suspected, God forgive me, that my friend didn't limit himself to theorizing about occultism, and that his intellectual diet, like his severe self-assurance, implied implementation, but he never was frank about this point and I have been discreet in my turn.

Chumming around with us, a little before the events I am about to narrate unfolded, was a young doctor, who only needed to pass his general examinations, in order to practice medicine; a profession he never pursued, as he has since given himself over completely to philosophy; and this was the other confidante who shared in the momentous revelation.

During the course of one of his long, intermittent vacations, we were separated from our inventor friend. On his return, we found him somewhat more nervous than usual, but radiant with a singular inspiration, and his first act was to invite us to a sort of philosophical salon - those were his words - where he would elucidate for us his latest discovery.

In his cramped, toilworn laboratory, which bore a vague resemblance to a locksmith's shop, and where there was always a whiff of chloroform in the air, the conference began.

With his steady, clear voice, his negligent demeanor, and his hands spread over the desk like a medium's during a séance, our friend made this startling announcement: "I have discovered the mechanical power of sound.

You know enough about these things," he proceeded, without concerning himself with the effect caused by his claim, "to understand that I'm not talking about the supernatural. It's a great find, certainly, but not superior to the discovery of Hertz's wave or Roentgen's ray.

By-the-bye, I have given a name to my force. As it is the last in the vibratory complex whose other components are heat, light and electricity - I call it the 'Omega Force'."

"But isn't sound a self-contained entity," asked the young doctor.

"No, since light and electricity are now considered as matter. That leaves heat; but by adopting the same analogy, we can confidently surmise its nature, and the day is coming when this postulate will confirm for all the world what is already plainly evident to me: that if bodies dilate when heated or, in other terms, if their intermolecular spaces expand, it's because among them something has been introduced and this something is heat. Moreover, when that heat is removed or dissipated, a body will revert to its former state because a vacuum is abhorred by nature and by reason.

For me, sound is matter; but this can be better seen from a proper exposition of my discovery.

The idea, intense but vague until the breakthrough occurred, came to me, oddly enough, the first time that I saw a bell being tuned. It is obvious that the precise note a bell will strike cannot be determined beforehand, since founding will change its tone. Once founded, it's necessary to trim the mouth, a process subject to two rules: if you want to lower the tone, the midline ridge, called the 'counterfeiter', must be diminished; to raise it, it's necessary to trim the 'paw' or, rather, the outer lip, and the tuning is done by ear, as with a piano. You can lower the sound even a full tone, but you cannot raise it except by half; if the paw is reduced too much, the bell will lose its sonority.

When I began to analyze how it is lost, I came to the conclusion which forms the basis of my discovery: a bell quits ringing not simply because it stops vibrating, but because the sonic vibration turns into mechanical force and stops being sound; but this only occurred to me during vacation, acquiring definition with solitude and concentration.

While I was engaged in modifying phonograph records I was involuntarily drawn towards the idea. I had been thinking of building a special type of tuning fork to test, by direct perception, the harmonies of the human voice, which isn't ordinarily possible except by means of a piano, and even then with marked inaccuracy; when suddenly, with such lucidity that, in two night's work, I conceived my entire theory, the facts presented themselves.

When a tuning fork strikes a tone, the prongs vibrate for sometime, which proves that the sound wave or, put differently, the agitated air, has sufficient force to move metal. Given the relationship which exists between the weight, density, and tensility of this instrument with those of air, the force exerted must be enormous; and nevertheless, it isn't capable of moving a sliver of straw that the slightest human breath could blow away, while breath, in its turn, is powerless to vibrate metal in any perceptible way. The sound wave is, then, more or less powerful than our own breaths. It depends on the circumstances; in the case of tuning forks, the circumstance must involve a molecular relationship and, if the reciprocals are not aligned and do not operate in unison, the phenomenon will be flawed, and fail to manifest. We have, then, to attribute sonic force to intermolecular phenomena.

Comprehension of this concept requires little ingenuity. Everyone has felt pulsations in the air made by very low sounds, those produced by the nasards of a pipe organ, for example. It seems that the sixteen vibrations per second generated by a pipe thirty-two feet in length marks the lowest limit of sound perceptible without a hum. With weaker vibrations, the movement turns into a gust of air; the gust moves the reed, but it doesn't affect the tuning fork. These low vibrations, genuinely melodious wisps of wind, are what make the windows tremble in cathedrals; but they don't form any notes, properly speaking, and only serve to reinforce the immediately superior octaves.

The higher the sound, the greater its resemblance to the wind and the more its wavelength is curtailed; but if it is considered as an intermolecular force, it is tremendously potent in the shrillest musical instruments; that of a piano hitting the seventh do, which attains a maximum of 4,200 vibrations per second, has a wave of three inches. The flute, which reaches 4,700 vibrations, makes a gigantic wave.

The wavelength depends, then, on the height of the sound, which stops being musical a little beyond the aforementioned 4,700 vibrations. So far I have been able to register a do, which turned out to be the tenth, at 32,770 vibrations, produced by the resonating arc of a minuscule tuning fork. I still perceive sound, but am unable to determine its musical structure, throughout the 45,000 vibration range of the tuning fork that I have invented.

"45,000 vibrations!" I said, "This is stupefying!"

"Soon you will see for yourselves," continued the inventor. "Be patient a moment longer." And, after offering us tea, which we declined, he said, "The sonic vibration, which becomes almost horizontal at high frequencies, while at the same time tending to lose its curvilinear form, reassumes a zig-zag pattern as the dissipating sound plays itself out. This has been experimentally demonstrated using a violin. Up to this point, we have not departed from common knowledge.

But as I've been saying, my intention was to study sound as a force. Here, then, is my theory, which rigorous research has subsequently borne out: the lower the sound, the more superficial are its effects on bodies. In view of all we have established, this is straightforward enough. The penetrational power of sound depends on its height and, as I have stated, a minor oscillation produced by my sound wave of 45,000 vibrations per second, is like an arrow which is scarcely quivering. As slight as this oscillation may be, it's always excessive, molecularly speaking and, since my tuning forks could not be refined any further, it was necessary to devise an alternative.

There was, moreover, another setback. The shape of the sound wave bears a relationship to its propagation, in such a way that it snowballs with increasing momentum until it encircles itself with sound, rendering impossible, in the process, the dispersal of its force; but this state is so untenable, as is the oscillation accompanying it, that the speed of the wave multiplies at an inconceivable rate, producing an effect of spontaneous disappearance. This depends on the wave not losing its horizontality; and, as every curve has to start somewhere, I inferred from these clues the existence of a corresponding scientific law.

Fourier, the celebrated French mathematician, has elaborated a principle applicable to simple waves - those pertinent to my problem - which can be crudely translated in this way: every complex wave form is compounded from a combination of simple waves of different lengths.

That being so, I conjectured that if I could initiate a series of whatever number of waves in proportional progression, the velocity of the first would equal the sum of the velocities of all of them together, and that, therefore, the ratio between the oscillation of the wave and its intermolecular transmission would indicate a break off point at which was liberated, at the same time, the mechanical power of sound.

My apparatus will demonstrate to you that all this is possible; but I still haven't fully explained my plan.

I consider that sound is matter, splintering off in infinitesimal particles from any primary sonic entity and made dynamic in the form of the sensation of sound, like the odoriferous particles which give the sensation of smell. This matter breaks off in the oscillatory form confirmed by science and engendering the aerial wave familiar to us, in the same way that the undulation of an eel underwater is repeated on the water's surface.

When the double wave collides with a solid body, the aerial portion is deflected by the surface; the ether, however, penetrates, producing the vibration in the body, and the ether in the body is then aligned with the harmonic dynamic of the wave diffused by it; and this is the explication, given here for the first time, of unisonous vibration.

Once the relationship between oscillation and propagation is disrupted, the sonoriferous ether spreads through the body's structure, thoroughly permeating it. And here's how: every body has a nucleus formed by the gravitation of molecules that hold it together, and which represents the total weight of said molecules. This nucleus may be situated in any part of the body. Molecules are configured in the same way as planetary masses in space.

It's clear that the most minimal displacement of the nucleus in question will instantly occasion the disintegration of the body; but it's no less certain that, to defy molecular cohesion, an enormous force is required; something of which the present day physicist or mechanical engineer has no conception, but which I have discovered, nevertheless.

Tyndall has said, in a graphic example, that the force of a fistful of snow contained in the hand of a child, would be enough to make a mountain fly into pieces. You can estimate what would be necessary to control this force. And I have disintegrated blocks of granite a cubic meter thick…"

He said this so casually, as if it were the most natural thing in the world, without bothering to acknowledge our baffled acquiescence. We were troubled, however nebulously, by the imminence of some great revelation; but, accustomed to the authoritative tone of our friend, we simply stood there, aghast and speechless. Our eyes scoured the workshop, brashly seeking the mysterious apparatus. Unless it might be the targetlike disk suspended from the apex of a metal tripod, nothing could be seen with which we weren't familiar.

"We have now arrived," continued our inventor, "at the final stage of the exposition. After having determined that it would be necessary to generate susceptible sound waves in proportional progression, and after spending many hours at the blackboard revising equations which I won't bore you by enumerating, I struck pay dirt.

There were the do, fa, sol, do, that, according to ancient tradition, constituted the lyre of Orpheus, and which contained the most important rhythmic units of declamation, which is to say, the musical secret of the human voice. The relationship of these waves mathematically is 1, 4/3, 3/2, 2; and, transcending nature, invulnerable to adulteration or deformity, they also, are an immanent force. So it must be apparent to you that the logic of the facts fits hand in glove with the theory.

I then proceeded to build my apparatus and, prior to developing the device which brings you here," he said, pulling from his pocket a thick disk resembling a nickel watch, "I tried a number of versions."

I confess that the apparatus left us nonplussed. All this business about the relationship of acoustic magnitudes mediated in some fashion, mentally, by human agency, and the talk about enormous forces and grandiose machines was a bit much to take. The cylindrical chest with a lever jutting from it, which now was unveiled before us, seemed to be something less than a generator of vibratory ether.

"First," continued the other, smiling at our perplexity," I thought in complex terms, along the lines of Koenig's sirens. Later, I simplified in accordance with my ideas concerning the shortcomings of machines, until I hit upon a temporary solution.

The delicacy of the cylinder does not permit it to be left opened at all times, as I'm sure you'll understand," he went on unscrewing the lid.

It contained four tiny tuning forks, not much bigger than bristles, implanted at unequal intervals in a wooden diaphragm that doubled as the bottom of the chamber. An ultra-thin filament dangled and distended, grazing them, under the action of the lever mounted above; and a cigar holder-sized mouthpiece formed the trumpet of a microphone.

"The gaps between the tuning forks, like the space needed for the play of the filament brushing them, impose on the apparatus its compact size," the inventor continued. "When they sound, the quadruple wave is transformed into one, and is expelled through the microphonic trumpet like an etheric missile. The discharge repeats itself as often as the lever is depressed, making it possible for the waves to leave without appreciable disruption of continuity, which is to say, much closer together than the bullets of a machine gun, and to form a veritable gusher of dynamic ether whose potency is incalculable.

If the wave travels to the molecular nucleus of a body, it disintegrates the nucleus into impalpable particles. If not, it will perforate the body with an almost imperceptible little hole. As for the tangential friction, you will come to see its effects on that disk..."

"What does it weigh," I interrupted.

"Three hundred kilograms."

The lever was engaged and the cylinder began to actuate with a dry, intermittent whirr. Our curiosity was exceeded only by incredulity and, so momentous was the silence, that we could barely discern a strident keening, resembling the buzzing of an insect.

Rapidly, the whole mass was set in motion, and sped up in such a manner that the whole house shook as if battered by a hurricane. The massive noise was no more than an errant shadow, like the sound made by the wings of a hovering hummingbird, and the air it displaced provoked a turbillion inside the room.

After awhile our inventor shut off his apparatus, which showed no visible strain or fatigue from its efforts, and with no change in the appearance of the tripod and its disk.

We gawked for a long while, held in suspense by a mixture of admiration and fear, unabashedly awed by this outlandish curiosity.

The doctor wanted to repeat the experiment but, apart from eliciting a little fluttering from the cylinder, nothing happened. I tried myself with the same results.

We had begun to think our friend had made a joke, when he said, so solemnly that he almost seemed sinister, "This is the mystery of my force. No one, not even I, can direct it. And I myself don't know how it works.

The best way I can describe what happens is to compare it to a gunshot. Without seeing it, without perceiving it in any material form, I know where to zero in on the nucleus I want to disintegrate, and I project my ether in the same form against the trembling target.

I have shown you what I've been attempting to achieve. Perhaps in the end, someday..."

Everything had been in vain. The etheric wave had dispersed futilely. As if to console himself or perhaps, to prove how close he had come to his goal, he invited us to stand witness as he executed a series of wonders.

A paving stone propping open the stubborn door disintegrated before our eyes, transforming itself, with a slight shudder, into a mountain of impalpable powder. Bands of steel suffered the same fate. The impression created by all this was of a magical mutation of matter, without perceptible effort, without a sound, except for the faint whine of a stifled murmur.

The doctor, bursting with enthusiasm, wanted to write an article.

"No," said our friend. He detested notoriety, although he couldn't avoid it completely; for then the neighbors began to come by. They demanded to know the cause of the disturbance...

"Well," he said; as if preparing them for something shocking.

"You haven't tried this on some animal," asked the doctor.

"You know," replied our friend with grave meekness, "that I could never cause pain to any living being ."

And with this the session ended.

The following days elapsed amidst marvels; and I remember as particularly noteworthy, the disintegration of a glass of water, which completely vanished, covering the entire workroom with mist.

The glass remained, explained the sage, because it didn't form a block with the water, which was unrestrained even by the perfect crystal adhesion. The same thing would happen if the glass were hermetically sealed. The liquid, converted into etheric particles, would be projected through the pores of the crystal…

Thus we went from astonishment to astonishment. The secret could no longer be kept, and it is impossible to evaluate the importance of what was lost as a consequence of the sad event whose telling will finalize this story.

What's certain is - if you are entertained by sad things - that one morning we found our friend, dead, with his head reclining against the back of his armchair.

It's easy to imagine our consternation. The amazing apparatus was in front of him, and nothing abnormal was noticed in the laboratory.

We gazed in surprise, at a complete loss to guess the cause of this disaster, when we suddenly noticed the wall which the dead man's head almost touched was covered with a grimy film.

At nearly the same time my companion noticed it, too, and, scraping his finger over this mixture, exclaimed in surprise, "It is cerebral matter … cerebellar cortex!"

The autopsy confirmed what he had said, verifying a new capacity of the portentous apparatus. Evidently, the head of our poor friend had emptied; not an atom of brains was left. The etheric projectile, who knows by what freak of direction or by what carelessness, had disintegrated his cerebellum, expelling it in an atomic explosion through the pores of his skull. Nary an external trace, on his person or on his clothes, betrayed what had happened, and this phenomenon, in all its horror was, I believe, the most stupendous of all those we had witnessed.

On the work bench, to bring the story to a close, was the gleaming apparatus, sitting ominously, within reach of my hand.

It functioned perfectly; but the formidable ether, the prodigious and homicidal substance of which I have such tangible and disgraceful proof, was lost, lost without a compass in the void of intermolecular space, in spite of all my futile efforts. At the Lutz and Schultz Institute they also tried, with null results.

# Origins of the Flood

## *Spirit Narrative*

The earth had attained a primal state of solid encrustation and found itself perpetually wreathed by a murky incandescence. Oceans of carbonic acid battered its continents of aluminum and lithium, then these became the first solids forming the terrestrial skin. Sulfur and boron also pumped through its tenuous veins.

The entire globe glistened like a monstrous silver ball. The atmosphere was of phosphorous with vestiges of chlorine and flourine. Flames of sodium, of silica, of magnesium shot forth, the luminous progeny of metals. This atmosphere glittered like a star, outspread across a span of many millions of miles.

On the continents and in their contiguous seas, organized life already flourished, if in guises inconceivable today; calcium phosphate didn't exist, and these beings had no bones. Oxygen and nitrogen which, along with a few traces of barium, figured in the composition of such life forms, made up the only fourteen constituent elements of the planet. Thus, everything in it was of an extreme simplicity.

The activity of those beings which possessed intelligence, however, was no less intense than at present, if of much lower amplitude; and the earth's complement of mollusks lived, worked, and felt in a manner analogous to that of today's humans. They came, for example, to construct enormous dwellings among lithium rock clusters; and the slime which sweated from their bodies oxidized aluminum in flaky filaments which glowed like incandescent asbestos.

Their bland structure was a consequence of the barely solid medium from which they sprang, and was adapted to the slight specific gravity of the continents they inhabited. They also possessed an amphibious aptitude; but as they had to resist certain temperatures and maintain themselves in definite forms under the pressure of the profound atmosphere, their structure derived support from its own fluidity.

Sketchy foreshadowings of men - more than men, properly speaking - a species of giant, hulking apes, had the ability to curl themselves up into compact gelatinous balls, or to expand like fantasms until almost turning into gaseous mist. The latter capacity had to do with absorption and touch, so that when it was necessary to incorporate objects into themselves, they could completely wrap around and envelop them, so as to feel them. Their hyperacute bipolar vision enabled them to function like veritable somnambulists. They lacked smell, taste, and hearing. They were formidable and perverse, these poor monsters of primeval creation. The lifespan of these beings, who knew how to ooze injurious organisms from their bodily fluids, was brief but noxious, like carrion with its worms. These were the giants of which the legends speak.

They built their cities the way snails build their shells, so that each dwelling was a kind of cloak exuded by its inhabitant. The houses were looped together by groups of vaulted archways, and their cities looked like clusters of brilliant clouds. They were almost that high, but not deployed in the blue sky, because blue didn't exist then, since the air lacked it. The atmosphere was colored only orange and red.

Scarcely two or three species of birds, whose wings had no feathers, but scales like those of butterflies, and whose coloring presaged then-nonexistent gold, mounted into the phosphorous atmosphere.

The sweep of the atmosphere was so lofty, and the flights of these birds so vast that they nearly reached the moon. The magnetic pull of the dead orb was the only thing that could ensnare them and as this then possessed an atmosphere in contact with the earth's, they sometimes approached it with impetuous boldness, and fell inanimate upon its fields of ice.

A vegetation of fungus and of gigantic lichens took hold on the earth's slippery terrain; next came the animals, never far behind in the primitive confusion of life's origins; some learned how to propel themselves by means of tentacles; others, though lacking spines, had birdlike beaks which opened and closed; others phosphoresced with friction; others spawned virtual spiders which went abroad and layed eggs from which germinated new versions of their vegetable progenitors. Especially dangerous were the electric cacti, which learned to project their needles.

The terrestrial elements stirred in a perpetual state of instability. They rose and crumbled, surged and sank, only momentarily blundering into concretion. Enormous geophysical pressures barely let these bodies solidify. Rocks which actually managed to form slept the sleep of inexistence. Precious stones were nothing but colors in the bands of the spectrum.

Such was the state of things before the catastrophe men afterwards called the flood; but this wasn't a pluvial or pelagic inundation, even if it was the cause of an influx of elemental liquid. The watery intervention took another form.

Now then: it's known that chemical elements, under certain circumstances, can, with the exception of weight, vary in specific characteristics until losing them almost altogether; and this is what is called allotropy. The classic example of red phosphorous and white phosphorous must be remembered here: the white, hungry for oxygen, is toxic and dissolves at 44 degrees centigrade; the red is almost indifferent to oxygen, innocuous and indissoluble, and this doesn't take into account other characteristics which accentuate the difference. Nevertheless, they are both forms of the same element, not to mention the diverse varieties of iron, or of silver, which also have allotropic configurations.

This is not to overlook, on the other hand, that heat multiplies the affinities of matter, making possible, for example, combinations of nitrogen and of carbon with other elements, something which doesn't happen at ordinary temperatures; and it is universally accepted, what is more, that the mere presence in an element of enough particles belonging to other elements can serve to change its properties or impart new ones. Particularly interesting in this respect is what happens to aluminum when put in contact with mercury. The mere shock of the collision causes it to oxidize until it dries up; being attacked by nitric and sulfuric acids, its water dissipates, and it is completely revised from that which it was before the contact took place.

To these causes of elemental variability, it's necessary to add pressure, able by and of itself to disintegrate solids to the point of liquefying them, whatever their malleability, steel included; pressure alone can convert it into a rubbery mass, which can be manipulated with total ease.

Finally, mention must be made of a strange property which chemists call catalytic action or, in vulgar terms, the action of presence, by means of which certain elements provoke others to combine, without taking part in those combinations themselves. Among these, one of the most active, and that which intervenes in the majority of cases, is water vapor. The foregoing data has been supplied simply in order to elucidate the larger phenomenon central to the present discussion.

After awhile it came to pass that the terrestrial atmosphere, condensing as the earth revolved, began to exercise an increasing attraction over the atmosphere of the moon. At the end of a certain period, the lunar atmosphere could no longer resist this attraction, and the earth began to incorporate the lightest elements of the moon's atmosphere with its own. The lack of pressure caused by this phenomenon vaporized the seas of the moon which were frozen many eons ago; and a cold mist, at many degrees below our thermometric zero, surrounded the dead satellite like a handkerchief.

One day the enormous reservoir of aqueous vapor, which had built up until it could no longer be contained, broke open, saturating the terrestrial atmosphere with a relentless influx of precipitation, augmenting its weight by countless millions of tons. To this phenomenon, the catalytic action of steam was added, and that was when terrestrial solids began to disintegrate.

A progressive softening endowed everything with the consistency of yeast; but as the phenomenon persisted, yeast soon turned into a kind of mud, triggering the catastrophe. Mountains were crushed under their own weight, and quickly degenerated into sand dunes which the wind ravished and demolished. The mansions of the giants crumbled to dust in their turn, and soon they observed with horror that their largely liquid habitat began to change in the most extraordinary manner; it dried up without disappearing, also turned to dust by the breakdown of its molecules, which had conglomerated with those of all the other elements to form a single, undifferentiated aggregate, simultaneously dry and fluid - without odor, color, or temperature.

The odd thing was that this phenomenon didn't affect all organisms in the same way. Some were more resistant, undoubtedly because of their semiliquid makeup; while other creatures quickly suffered violent death in this dispersion. Soon nothing existed on the globe but the flotsam borne adrift on these shifting cosmic sands; the majority of animate beings had died from inanition; although they couldn't eat as we do, they absorbed their vital sustenance from the air, and the air was changed by the influence of the moon.

First one, then another great mollusk sank beneath the waveless universal flood, beneath the horror of the titanic atmosphere, impregnated with mortal toxins, where the future was taking shape. They could muster but scant resistance to such environmental fluctuations, and this inability to adapt took its toll. They, too, were dispersed, even to the point of extinction; and then, over the ambit of the planet, fell a mantle of solitude and blackest night.

Thousands of years later, the elements began to recompose.

Formidable chemical tempests raged until they reached a state of critical mass, and the fourteen primitive elements revived and assumed new combinations.

Lithium was triplicated in potassium, rubidium and cesium;

phosphorous in arsenic, antimony and bismuth; carbon generated titanium and zirconium; sulfur, selenium and tellurium…

The oceans were already filled with water, water from the moon periodically exalted when its origin was made known by the oceans' harmonic dilation. The atmosphere had been distilled into air like ours, although permeated with carbonic acid.

No living being was left from the prior creation. Even their footprints had been erased. But the vapors of the moon appareled themselves with living germs, so that the new state of the earth was slowly called into existence.

The sea covered itself with rudimentary life. The solid crust sprouted grasses, and the dominion of these lasted an age.

But I will not belabor the matter by detailing the enormous process. It only remains to say that the first human beings were organized from water: beautiful monsters, half fish, half women, later called sirens in mythology. They dominated the secret of the original harmony, and adorned the planet with melodies of the moon which contained the secret of death.

Their flesh was white like that of their maternal orb; and the primitive sodium that pervaded their new element of existence engendered noble metals, and garlanded their tresses with a gold even then unknown…

…And thus have you called forth my memories, across millions of years, evoking human sentiment, summoning me here to speak from the dimension where I dwell - the earth's cone of shadow. For there I am condemned to abide, throughout the ages, so long as the planet endures.

✳✳✳

The medium fell silent, wearily reclining her head on the shoulder of the sofa. And Mr. Skinner, one of the eight persons sitting in the session, could not restrain himself from blurting in the half-light:

"The cone of shadow! The flood!…What outlandish fakery! What charlatanism!"

None of us said anything to dispute him, when a disturbance coming through the medium distracted us.

From her left side descended a tenebrous mass, plainly perceptible in the penumbra. It grew into a huge globule, projecting from its midsection a number of long, slithering tentacles and, once fully articulated, detached itself and dropped onto the floor like a giant spider. Next it dilated itself until it filled the room and engulfed us like glue, pulsing rhythmically and gurgling with a low, murmurous groan. It didn't have definite form in the darkness densened by its presence; but if horror can be objectified in some fashion, this was horror.

No one dared budge before the frightful formication of shadowy tentacles which loomed all around us, and there's no telling what would have happened next if the medium hadn't implored in a fainting voice:

"Light! In God's name, light!"

I bounded for the light switch and fumbled for the toggle; as the light snapped on, the shadowy mass burst like a bubble, whooshing into thin air like an enormous expulsion of breath.

We stared in silence.

We were completely covered by something like congealed mud; and this would have been enough of a shock if Skinner, offering to help to clean up the mess, hadn't made still more startling a discovery while rinsing out a pail.

In the bottom of the wash basin, no bigger than a drowned rat, but finished in form and beauty, radiating a mortal whiteness, was a little dead siren.

# The Horses of Abdera

On the coast of the Aegean lay the Thracian city of Abdera, now called Balastra, which should not be confused with its Andalusian namesake, and which was celebrated far and wide for its horses.

In Abdera, to excel at horse breeding was no small feat, since Abdera's distinction in this area was unsurpassed. Every inhabitant took personal pride in husbanding these noble animals; and this passion, cultivated obstinately over the course of many generations, until it formed one of the region's fundamental traditions, had produced marvelous results. The horses of Abdera enjoyed exceptional fame, and the entire Thracian populace from the Cicilians to the Bisaltars, paid tribute to the Bithynians, founders of Abdera. What's more, this flourishing enterprise of horse rearing, which was a matter of sport as much as commerce, busied everyone from the King to the humblest citizen.

These circumstances fostered an unusual closeness in the relationship between the brutes and their masters, much more than was customary among other nations, so that the stable came to be regarded as a household annex, and this enthusiasm even extended to admitting horses at the dining table.

They were truly extraordinary steeds, but beasts just the same.

Some slept in the finest silk sheets; others had mangers adorned with simple frescoes, since many veterinarians maintained that the equine race was endowed with refined aesthetic tastes, and the equine cemetery boasted, among the overwrought, run-of-the-mill monuments, two or three genuine masterpieces. The most beautiful temple in the city had been consecrated to Arion, the horse that Neptune caused to spring from the earth with a jab of his trident; and it was believed that the fashion for finishing ships' prows with horses' heads, had the same origins; equine bas reliefs, in any case, were unquestionably the most common ornament in their architecture. The King's own devotion to horses was unqualified, even to the point of pardoning their crimes, which had the effect of making them singularly fierce, so that the names of Podargus and Lightning Bolt figured in somber fables, for Abderan horses, it should be remarked, were given names like people.

So well-trained were these animals that bridles were unnecessary; they were kept only for decorative purposes, much appreciated by the horses themselves. The spoken word was the usual medium of communication with them, and it should be observed that the complete freedom afforded them brought out their best behavior; they were allowed to roam wherever they wished, unsaddled and unharnessed, and to graze amongst the lush pastures set aside for their use, along the banks of the River Kossinites, or in the other special preserves allotted for their nourishment and recreation.

At the sound of a trumpet, they gathered when needed, and were most punctual whether for work or for the feed trough. Verging on the incredible was their flair for all sorts of circus acts and even parlor tricks, their bravery in combat, their discretion at solemn ceremonies. Thus, the Hippodrome of Abdera became famous not only for its tightrope walkers, but for its horses armored in bronze and for its opulent funerals, attaining such reknown that people came from everywhere to gape in awed admiration at both trainers and steeds alike.

This persistent education, this enforced maintenance of encouraging conditions and nurturing support and, to put it in one word, this humanization of the equine race, began to engender a phenomenon that the Bithynians celebrated as another national glory: the intelligence of the horses began to blossom along with their consciousness, producing aberrations which stimulated no end of public discussion and debate.

A mare demanded mirrors for her stall and, after tearing them off the walls of her master's bedroom with her teeth, she trampled the mirrors to bits, when he got upset. When her master at last gave in to her caprice, she became a perfect coquette. Panic, an elegant and high-strung Palomino, and the most handsome stallion in the district, who had two military campaigns behind him, and who rejoiced at the recital of heroic hexameters, died broken-hearted for love of a woman. She was the wife of a general, the mistress of the enamored brute, and the lady did nothing to hide what had happened. It was generally believed that the curious crush gratified her vanity, and no one thought the worse of the affair, since occurences of this sort were commonplace in the equestrian capitol.

There was an outbreak of equine infanticide, with the number of cases mounting to an alarming degree, until it became necessary to forestall them by allowing foals to be adopted by elderly mules. The horses exhibited an increasing appetite for fish and for hemp, and they led the other animals on raids of the plantations, and sporadic uprisings of horses against their masters had to be corrected by hot pokers, the lash proving an insufficient deterrent. This harsh expedient was employed more and more as the spirit of rebellion spread like wildfire among the unruly animals.

The Bithynians, more enraptured than ever with their beloved horses, paid no real heed to this situation. There were soon more serious incidents. Two or three teams of horses mobbed together in an attack on a drayman who had whipped an uncooperative mare. More and more the horses resisted the bit and the yoke, until donkeys began to be used in their place. There were animals who refused to accept any livery or tack at all, but their refractory behavior was indulged by their wealthy owners, who preferred to laugh away the insurrection as if it were all an amusing whim.

One day the horses failed to approach when the trumpet summoned, and it was necessary to round them up by force and, after this latest episode, the rebellion seemed to have been quelled.

Some time later, as it turned out, the beach was littered with dead fish which the tide had washed up, as had often happened in the past. The horses glutted themselves on this gratuitous maritime bounty and, when they were sated, sauntered back to the suburban meadows with ominous slowness.

It was at midnight that the extraordinary conflict erupted.

Suddenly a deafening and persistent thunderclap rumbled through the outskirts of the city. It was all of the horses stampeding at once in order to assault it; but this wasn't learned until later. All that was noticed at first was an unusual rustling noise, whose nature couldn't be discerned in the nighttime darkness; no one had suspected that a surprise attack might be imminent.

As the pasturelands were within the city walls, the main wave of the assault went unopposed; and because the animals had intimate knowledge of their masters' domiciles, the devastation was appalling.

As eventful as the night was, its outrages became fully apparent only when daylight revealed its evidence, compounding the horrors of the night before. Doors had been bashed in by hoofblows, and lay on the ground, smashed, offering no resistance to the frantic hordes of horses which streamed in furiously in an uninterrupted flood. The streets were dashed with blood, and not a few citizens fell crushed beneath the flashing hooves and gnashing teeth of the stormy band whose ranks wreaked further havoc by turning man's own weapons against him.

Shaken to its foundations by the rampaging herds, the city darkened with the dust they engendered; and a strange tumult formed by screams of rage or stifled shrieks of despair mingled with whinnyings as subtle as speech, while the stampings of hooves on the battered doors added to the weird hideousness of the catastrophe. A kind of incessant earthquake made the ground vibrate with the galloping hoofbeats of the rebellious mass, violently gusting at times into a hurricane of frenzied troops charging willy-nilly, without direction or objective. Having ransacked all the hemp fields, and taken their fill of the wine cellars they had coveted ever since they had first learned an appreciation for such luxuries of refined leisure, groups of intoxicated animals accelerated the pace of destruction. And it was impossible to flee to the seashore. The horses, knowing what the ships were for, had cut off access to the port.

Only the citadel had withstood the onslaught, and the men began to organize their resistance there. They fired arrows at any horse that came within range, and when one fell nearby, it was dragged inside to be eaten.

Among the besieged citizens the most extraordinary rumors circulated: that the first attack, for example, had not started out as a murderous spree, but merely a mischievous romp; that the horses had broken into the houses strictly in order to try on the sumptuous attire and the sparkling jewels, and that it was only when their designs were opposed that their fury was aroused.

Others spoke of monstrous acts of passion, of women assaulted and crushed in their own beds with bestial impetuosity; and there was even one noble lady who managed to stammer, between tearful outbursts, an account of her ordeal: of how she was awakened in her dimly-lit bedchamber in the middle of the night by the foul breath of a black colt who was rubbing his disgusting lips against hers, curling his ignoble muzzle, and baring his hideous teeth; her scream of terror before the crazed beast, eyes flashing with a human and malevolent gleam, inflamed with lust; and the sea of blood with which she was drenched after her servant ran it through with a sword…

They enumerated murders in which mares had diverted themselves with female fury, mangling their victims with vicious bites. They massacred the donkeys, and the mules joined in the melee, allying themselves with the horses, mindlessly destroying for the sake of destruction, and particularly delighting in trampling dogs.

The din made by the rebellious chargers resounded throughout the city, and the fragor of the riot swelled at every turn. If they didn't want to abandon the city to the most ruthless destruction, it was imperative for the defenders to organize some means of escape, even though the steadily increasing savagery of the assailants was drastically reducing prospects for success. The men mustered their arms; having tasted blood, the horses decided to attack again.

A sharp silence preceded the assault. From the fortress could be seen the terrible army that had assembled, not without effort, in the hippodrome. This process lasted for some hours but when everything seemed ready, a spontaneous surge of prancing and rearing, and of screech-like neighings whose meaning it was impossible to decipher, threw the horse ranks into ragged disarray.

The sun was already going down, when the first charge took place. It wasn't, if the phrase may be permitted, more than a show of force, since the animals limited their offensive to running en masse in front of the fortress. They returned riddled by arrows.

From the city's edge, they dashed forward once again, and the shock against the defenses was formidable. The entire citadel rocked and reverberated under the storm of thundering hooves, and the sturdy Doric columns bolstering the ramparts were severely strained.

The first wave was survived, but a second attack soon followed.

The most pernicious instruments of destruction were the shod horses and domesticated mules who fell by the dozen; but their ranks closed around them with maddened urgency, leaving the throng almost undiminished. The worst thing was that some of them had outfitted themselves with suits of armor against whose steel mail the arrows were blunted. Others wore strips of gaudy fabric or tinkling necklaces and, childlike in their tantrums, gaily burst into frisky frolics.

Some of them were recognized from the ramparts: Dinos, Aethon, Ameteo, Xanthos! They greeted their masters with jubilant whinnies, whisking their tails, then rearing up on their hind legs and kicking fiercely at the air with their forelegs. One, obviously a commander, stood up on his hind hocks, and strutted like this for a while, gracefully swaying his forelegs in the air as if dancing a martial minuet, and twisting his neck with serpentine elegance, until an arrow struck him straight through the heart.

The attackers, meanwhile, had victory within their grasp. The walls started to give way.

Suddenly an alarm paralyzed the beasts. One after another, propping themselves on the rumps and backs of their comrades, the horses stretched their necks in the direction of the poplar grove which bordered the banks of the Kossinites; and the defenders, swiveling their eyes in the same direction, were met with a terrifying spectacle.

Looming above the somber grove, awesome against the late afternoon sky, a colossal lion's head stared down on the city. It was one of those ferocious antediluvian creatures which, though nearly extinct, still, from time to time, devastated the Rhodopean mountains. Never had they seen anything more monstrous than this head which dominated the tallest trees, intertwining with the dangling, twilit leaves, the locks of its matted hair.

They could see its enormous fangs glistening in the sunlight, its eyes squinting in the glare, and the odor of its deadly scent was carried on the breeze. Motionless amidst the palpitating foliage, its gigantic, rust-colored mane gilded by the dazzling sun, it burgeoned on the horizon like one of those boulders on which Pelasgian, older than the hills, engraved his barbarous deities.

And suddenly it began to walk; slow as an ocean. From the parting branches its chest emerged, heaving with bellows-like breathing which would soon terrorize the city, no doubt, when it turned into a roar.

In spite of their strength and numbers, the insurgent horses couldn't endure the appearance of such a creature. With one body, they lunged towards the sea, in the direction of Macedonia, raising a veritable whirlwind of sand and spray, as not a few hurled themselves into the waves.

In the fortress panic reigned. What could they do against such an enemy? What bronze hinge could withstand such jaws? What wall withstand its massive claws?

Too worn out to reload their bows, they had already begun to prefer the earlier hazard (at least it was a struggle against civilized beasts), when the monster emerged from the trees.

It was not a growl which thundered from its throat, but a human battle cry, the bellicose "…ululuuu…" of combat, to which the rejoicing defenders' triumphant response of "all hail!" and "hip, hurrah!" rose from the fortress.

Oh, wondrous sight!

Beneath the feline skull, was the face of a god, radiating a

# Viola Acherontia

*W*hat this extraordinary gardener wanted to create was a flower of death. His experiments, conceived and carried out over the course of ten years, invariably yielded negative results. This was because he treated members of the vegetable kingdom as entities lacking a soul, a thing which always adheres to beings made of clay; and because he concentrated, therefore, strictly on his plants' corporeal composition. Grafts, mutations: he tried everything. Cultivation of the black rose busied him for a time; but nothing came of his investigations. Next, tulips and passionflowers held his interest, the upshot being two or three monstrous specimens; but he was getting nowhere until Bernardin de Saint-Pierre steered him onto a productive path, pointing out to him certain analogies between flowers and pregnant women, stemming from the assumption that both are capable of retaining at "whim", an imprint of the essence, and of the active principle, of a desired object.

Acceptance of this audacious postulate is tantamount to hypothesizing the existence in plants of a mental capacity sufficiently elevated to receive, concretize, and conserve an impression; in other words, of assigning to them a susceptibility to suggestion on a par with that of inferior animal organisms. It was precisely this which our gardener was determined to demonstrate.

According to him, the patterns of growth and the distribution of the stems, shoots, buds, and blooms of twining plants, such as the convolvulus, obeyed predetermined tendencies which could be precisely predicted and manipulated. Armed with the prerequisite know-how, it was a simple matter to train the seemingly capricious sprawl of stalks and stems, runners and roots, to conform to any configuration a gardener might care to devise. A simple nervous system presided over these obscure functions. Each plant also had its cerebral bulb and its rudimentary heart, situated respectively in the cortex of the root and in the trunk. In seed, that is to say, the being repeated by procreation, this can be seen with complete clarity. The embryo of a walnut has the same heart-shaped form as its core, and its cotyledons abundantly resemble its brainlike shell. The two rudimentary sprigs which sprout from this embryo distinctly remember and faithfully preserve the two lobelike branches whose functions they repeat in germination.

External morphological traits almost always presuppose internal similarities; and this shows that suggestion exercises a greater influence over the formation of organisms than is commonly believed. Some clairvoyants of natural history, including Michelt and Fries, long ago presented this truth which experiment has since confirmed. The world of insects proves it conclusively. Birds display more brilliantly colored plumage in countries whose skies are always clear (Gould). White cats and those with blue eyes are frequently deaf (Darwin). There are fish which carry photovoltaic cells in the gelatinous tissues of their dorsal fins, the electric eel being one example (Strindberg). The sunflower gazes constantly at the daystar, and faithfully reproduces its nucleus, its rays, and its spots (Saint-Pierre). And, in this same connection, a momentary digression is in order. Bacon, in his *Novum Organum,* established that the cinammon laurel and other odoriferous plants found in fetid places obstinately retain their aromas and refuse to emit them; they do this so as to keep from mixing themselves with noxious exhalations…

The experiment which the extraordinary gardener had conducted and whose aftermath he proposed to show me, involved suggestion over violets. He had found them singularly nervous, which predisposed them, he claimed, to those exaggerations of affection and horror hysterics are given to, and he wanted to make them discharge a mortal poison without any odor: a fulsome yet imperceptible toxin. Though what he proposed to do with it, if it wasn't purely a macabre vagary, would always remain a mystery to me.

I found an old man, stricken in years, of unassuming demeanor, who received me with an almost humble courtesy. I was full of myself, and he was entertained by my naive pretensions, which served as inoffensive preliminaries to a lengthy conversation on the theme which had brought us together.

He loved his flowers like a father, and displayed fanatical devotion to them. The ideas outlined above formed the introduction to our dialog and, as the man found in me a fellow connoisseur, he blossomed with pride.

After expounding his theories to me with rare precision, he invited me to see his violets.

"I have managed," he said as we walked, "to breed a specimen whose leaves exhale a toxin derived from its own chemistry; and though the results have been imperfect, their behavior is nothing short of marvelous; especially considering that I had begun to despair of ever obtaining mortiferous exhalations. But I have done it. Let me show you."

The specimens were at the extreme edge of the garden, in a sort of small plaza crammed with strange plants. From among the usual verdure, somersaulted some striking corollas which at first I took for pansies, because they were black.

"Black violets," I exclaimed.

"Yes, that's right; I began with color, so that the funebrial idea would be better instilled in them. Black is, except in the case of Chinese fairy tales, the natural color of mourning, as well as that of night, which is to say of sadness, of vital diminution, and of dreams, brothers of death. What's more, these flowers have no scent, as I predicted, and this is yet another effect of the law of correlation. The color black appears to be, in fact, adverse to scent. Thus you have more than one thousand one hundred and ninety-three species of white flowers, of which there are one hundred and seventy-five scented and a dozen fetid ones; while of the more than eighteen species of black flowers, seventeen are inodorous and one fetid. But this is not the interesting thing about the subject. The marvelous thing is in another detail, which requires, unfortunately, a long explanation..."

"Don't worry," I replied, "my desire to learn is at least as great as my curiosity."

"Listen, then; this is what I did: first, I had to prepare for my flowers a medium favorable to promoting the funereal idea; later, this idea was suggested to them by a whole series of phenomena. After attuning their nervous systems to receive and fix images, I stimulated production of the poison by combining, in the violets' environment and in their sap, diverse vegetable venoms. Heredity takes care of the rest. The violets which you see belong to a family cultivated under this regimen over a ten year period. The development of some of the hybrids, indispensable for preventing degeneration, somewhat retarded the final outcome of my experiment. And I say final outcome because making a black, odorless violet is in itself a breakthrough.

Nevertheless, this isn't difficult; starting with a carbon base, I performed a succession of reductions with the object of obtaining a variety of aniline. Without enumerating all the steps and stages involved, and the interminable investigations of balsams and xylenes, whose enormous series took me far afield, suffice it to say that I arrived at the secret via a different route. Permit me, however, to divulge a hint: the origin of the color which we call aniline ensues from a combination of hydrogen and carbon; the chemical work behind it consists of reducing and stabilizing oxygen and nitrogen, to produce the artifical alkalis of the aniline type, from which derivatives are extracted afterwards. I've made something similar. You know that chlorophyll is very sensitive and, owing to this sensitivity, one more surprising result comes about. Exposing ivy plants to sunlight, in a place where the light is let in only by rhomboidal apertures, alters the shape of their leaves so persistently, that they adopt the geometric type known as a cissoid curve; and it's easy to observe that plots of grass creeping under a thicket, or on the floor of a forest, wind about in imitation of the arabesque patterns of light filtering through the branches…

We come now to the greatest challenge. Putting suggestion into effect over my flowers is very difficult, as plants have their brains underground: they are inverted beings. Because of this I created an artifical midnight, simulating perpetual darkness and maximizing exposure to this darkness as a fundamental element. I obtained the black color of the violets, and it was then that the first funebrial note was sounded. Next I planted, in the violets' vicinity, stramonium, jasmine, and belladonna. My flowers were thus constantly subject to these chemical and physiologically funebrial influences. Solanine is, in effect, a narcotic venom, which works in the same way as hyosycamine and atropine, the two pupil-dilating alkaloids contained in datura, which produce megalopsia, or the magnification of objects. So we now have, then, the properties of dream and hallucination, which is to say, the instigators of nightmares; and, in sum, the specific effects of the color black, of dreams, and of hallucinations, are brought together to incite fear. I hasten to add that, to amplify hallucinatory impressions, I planted henbane also, the active ingredient of whose poisonous root is hyosycamine."

"And how was this of any use to you, being as flowers have no eyes," I asked.

"Ah, Sir; we don't see only with our eyes," replied the old doctor. Somnambulists see with the fingers of their hands and with the soles of their feet. Don't forget that here we are treating suggestion."

My lips overflowed with objections; but he cut me short, summoning me to the spot where he had brought to fruition so singular a theory.

"Solanine and datura," proceeded my interlocutor, "closely approximate the fatal poisons ptomaine and leucomaine, which exhale odors of jasmine and rose. And while belladonna and stramonium lend the violets their toxic essences, the scent is supplied by jasmine and rose bushes whose perfume is intensified, according to the observations of Candolle, when onions are sown nearby. The cultivation of roses is now very advanced. Grafting has made their variations prodigious; in Shakespeare's time, the first roses in England were grafted…"

This anecdote which had obviously been contrived to flatter my literary inclinations, moved me nevertheless.

"Permit me," I said, "to admire, by the way, your remarkably youthful powers of retention."

"Further accentuating the influences over my flowers," he continued, smiling vaguely, "I have encircled them with the cadaverous narcotic plants. Some arum and orchids, a few stapelia here and there, whose colors and odors recall those of rotting flesh. Violets, overexcited by their naturally amorous disposition, given that the flower is an organ of reproduction, inhale the cadaverous poisons along with the corrupt fragrance of the cadaver itself; already predisposed to hypnosis, they readily suffer the soporific influence of the narcotics, and the hallucinatory, megalopsia-inducing properties of the pupil-dilating toxins. The funebrial suggestion begins thus to ingrain itself with consuming intensity; but all the time the abnormal sensitivity of the flowers is heightened through contact with these potent plants, straining to narrow the distance between themselves and a valerian shrub or shying away from a horseman's spurs whose cyanide notably irritates them. Ethyl of rose is also a collaborator here. We have now reached the culmination of the experiment, but before I show you the results, I would like to give this warning: the human ow! is a cry of nature."

Even apart from this last outburst of drivel, the unbalanced personality of my interlocutor was evident to me; but he, without giving me time to thoroughly think it through, went on:

"'Ow!' is, in fact, an interjection made by people all the time. But the curious thing is that, among animals, this happens, too. From the dog, a higher vertebrate, to the death's head moth, a lepidopter, 'ow!' is a manifestation of pain and of fear. The strange insect whose name derives from the fact that it carries the design of a skull on its thorax, is a good reminder of the lugubrious fauna in which the 'ow!' principle is common. Not to mention owls; but no list would be complete which didn't include that fantastically forlorn denizen of the primitive forests, the sloth, which seems to carry all the pained regret of its decadence in the sorrowful 'ow' which is his watch-word, and one of the sources of his fame…Taking all this into account, exasperated by my ten years of travail, I decided to act out, in front of the flowers, increasingly cruel scenes, striving more and more to engrave a forceful impression; still there was no progress until, one day…But, if you'll step over here, you may judge for yourself…"

His bent over the flowers, lowering his face until it almost touched them, and instructed me to do the same. Then, an amazing thing happened: I seemed to perceive a series of faint moans, of feeble laments. Suddenly I was convinced. These flowers sighed, in effect, and from their dark corollas rose a pullulation of little "ohs" very similar to those of a child. Suggestion had operated in a completely unforeseen fashion, and these flowers, during all their brief existence, did nothing but cry.

My stupefaction had been brought to a head, when suddenly a terrifying idea took hold of me. I remembered what was said in the legends of witchcraft, about how the mandrake also wept when it was sprinkled with the blood of child; and, harboring a suspicion which made me deathly pale, I brought it up.

"Like the mandrake," I said.

"Like the mandrake," he repeated, turning even more pale than I.

And I never went back to see him. My attitude now is to regard him as a virtual degenerate, as a perfect warlock of another era, with his poisons and his flowers of crime. Could I bring myself to duplicate the mortiferous violet he propounded? Should I tell how it was done?

# Yzur

*I* bought the ape at an auction of property from a bankrupt circus.

The first time it occurred to me to undertake the experiment outlined in these pages was one afternoon, while reading, I don't remember where, that the natives of Java attribute the lack of articulate language in monkeys to abstention, not to incapacity. "They abstain from talking," the book said, "so that humans will not make them work."

This idea, which at first didn't strike me as being particularly plausible, absorbed me more and more until it took the shape of a definite anthropological postulate: monkeys once were men who, for one reason or another, stopped speaking. This fact produced an atrophy of their phonetic organs and of the language centers in their brains, which were weakened almost to the point of ceasing to exist, leaving the sole idiom of the species an inarticulate screech, as the primitive human descended to the level of the animal.

Obviously, if this could be demonstrated, it would explain all the anomalies, quirks, and oddities that make the monkey such a fascinating creature; but there was only one possible way to make such a demonstration: to induce a monkey to resume the use of language.

In the meantime, I had traveled the globe with my pet, forming an ever closer bond through our many wanderings and adventures together. In Europe he drew a great deal of attention, and had I wished, I could have made him as famous as the celebrated simian showman, Jo-Jo, the Almost-Human, but my lifestyle as a serious businessman was ill-suited to such enterprises.

Pursuing my theories about monkeys and language, I pored over the entire bibliography concerning the problem, without appreciable results. All I knew for certain was that there was no scientific reason why monkeys shouldn't speak. But proving this was to take five years of constant study and thought.

Yzur (a name whose origins I was never able to discover, any more than was his former owner) was truly an extraordinary animal. His upbringing in the circus, and his training there, which was almost exclusively a matter of mimickry, had sharpened many of his faculties; and this inspired me all the more to test my apparently ludicrous ideas on him. It is known that the chimpanzee (which is what Yzur was) is the most intelligent and one of the most docile members of the monkey family, a fact which bolstered my chances. Every time I saw him approach on two feet, with his hands held behind his back to keep his balance, and his drunken sailor's swagger, my conviction that he was a lapsed human grew stronger.

There is no reason why a monkey should not utter articulate speech. His natural language, which is to say the conjunction of screeches with which he communicates to his fellows, is varied enough; his larynx, though differing from a human's, is not as different as a parrot's, and parrots speak quite well; and where his brain is concerned, even if the comparison with the parrot left any doubt, it should be remembered that the brain of an idiot also is underdeveloped, yet there are many cretins who can pronounce individual words. As for the significance of Brocas' convolution, this depends, clearly, on the total development of the brain; it has not been proven that this is conclusively the site of the localization of language. Even if anatomy has established no likelier location, the facts are far from certain.

Happily, monkeys possess, along with many bad traits, a taste for learning, as is readily shown by their imitative tendencies, which have their basis in a strong memory, powers of reflection which extend even to the practice of dissimulation, and an attention span comparatively more developed than a child's. The monkey is, in fact, an ideal pedagogic subject. What's more, my chimp was young, and it's known that monkeys pass through their highest phase of intelligence while juveniles. The only difficulty rested with the method to be employed in communicating with him in words.

I was aware of all the fruitless experiments of my predecessors; and it goes without saying, given the expertise of some of them, and the null results netted by their endeavors, that my own attempts were also bound to fail; but the problem kept gnawing at me, and I couldn't avoid the conclusion that: the first step must be to strengthen the monkey's phonic organs. This is, in effect, what is done with deaf mutes in the first stage of their instruction; no sooner had I begun to ponder this question, when the anologies between the deaf mute and the monkey came home to me with a vengeance. First of all, their extraordinary mimetic ability, which makes up for the absence of organized speech, shows that just because they don't speak doesn't mean they don't think, even though the latter faculty may have been dulled by the paralysis of the former. Then we must take into account other still more notable characteristics such as diligence in work, loyalty, and courage, unquestionably augmented by two propensities whose interdependence is as necessary as it is revealing: a gift for feats of balance, and a resistance to nausea and vertigo.

So I decided to launch my efforts with a series of elementary lip and tongue exercises, treating Yzur as if he were a deaf mute. I was wagering that once he had graduated this phase of the training, he would depend on his hearing to establish direct associations with words, without needing to revert to gestures. As it turned out, I was being over-optimistic in playing such a hunch.

Fortunately, of all the great apes, the chimpanzee has the most flexible lips, and in this particular case, Yzur, who suffered from throat infections, knew how to open his mouth for medical examinations. The first inspection confirmed my suspicions, at least in part. Yzur's tongue stayed at the bottom of his mouth, an inert mass, evidencing no movements except those attending the act of swallowing. Vocal training produced the desired effect and, after two months, he had learned to stick out his tongue as a joke. This was the first time I was able to observe a relationship between the movement of his tongue and an idea; a relationship in perfect accord with his nature, I might add.

The lips took a lot of work, and I even had to manipulate them, pinching or stretching them with tweezers, but, perhaps because of my expression, he appreciated the importance of the strange task, and applied himself to it dutifully. Meanwhile I demonstrated lip movements for him to imitate, while he sat there, scratching his rump with his hand twisted behind his back, and blinking in puzzled concentration, or stroking his hairy cheeks with all the airs of a man organizing his thoughts by means of rhythmic gesticulation. Finally he learned to move his lips.

But linguistic skills are slow to form, as is easily seen in the protracted period of babbling undergone by infants and toddlers, whose acquisition of speech parallels their intellectual development. Indeed, language production is controlled by the speech center of the brain, and the two must work side by side, in collaborative harmony, if normal development is to occur. This linkage was elaborated in 1785 by Heinicke, the inventor of the oral method for teaching deaf mutes, with philosophical consequences. He spoke of a "dynamic concatenation of ideas", a phrase whose profound clarity would do honor to a contemporary psychologist.

Yzur found himself, respecting language, in the same situation as a child who, before actually speaking learns many words; but, because of his broader range of life experiences and his familiarity with a diversity of objects, he was much more adroit at making connections and choices. These choices must have been based not merely on the retention of impressions, but on inquisitiveness and comparative analysis, to judge by their variety and, as it must be assumed that there is some form of abstract reasoning involved in this process, I had to conclude that Yzur had a superior degree of intelligence undoubtedly favorable to my investigations.

If my theories seem overly daring, it should be pointed out that the syllogism, which is the fundamental basis of logical argument, it is not foreign to the mentality of many animals. After all, the syllogism was originally a comparison between two sensations. If not, why do some animals flee from men when they see him, while those who have never seen men do not?

Next I began Yzur's phonetic education.

First I tried to teach him the mechanics of verbalization, before progressing to meaningful words. Monkeys hold an advantage over deaf mutes in that they not only have a voice, but have an excellent innate capacity for controlling rudimentary articulation. I tried to teach Yzur to modulate his voice in order to produce different sounds and phonemes; professors call these static or dynamic, according to whether they refer to vowels or consonants.

Given the gluttony of monkeys, I thought it might prove useful to employ a method implemented by Heinicke in his work with deaf mutes. I decided to associate each vowel with a tasty tidbit - a with potato, e with beet, i with pie, o with cocoa, u with prune - arranging matters so that the word for each tidbit contained a vowel which was either dominant and repeated as in cocoa, or a combination of vowels accented by both tonic and prosodic stresses, as in potato.

All went well when I tried out the vowels, since they are sounds formed by the open mouth. Yzur learned them in fifteen days. The u was the most difficult for him to pronounce. The consonants, on the other hand, were devilishly tricky. Slowly I came to the realization that he would never be able to enunciate the ones formed between the teeth and gums. His long front incisors simply ruled this out. Our vocabulary was reduced, then, to the five vowels and the consonants b, k, m, g, f, and c; that is, to those consonants whose formation required nothing but the tongue and the palate. Although even for this the aural method alone was not sufficient. He had to have recourse to gestures like a deaf mute, placing his hand on my chest and then on his own in order to feel the sonic vibrations made by the sounds.

And three years passed, without his uttering a single word. He exhibited a tendency to identify a thing according to the most dominant letter in its name. That was all.

In the circus, he had learned to bark, like the dogs who were his work companions; and when he saw me despair that my vain attempts would never succeed in getting him to speak, he would bark as loud as he could as if to show me all he knew. He would pronounce vowels and consonants separately, because he couldn't combine them. The best he could do was to string together a jabbering succession of m's and p's.

However slow the process, there gradually came a great change in his character. He flexed his facial features less and less, his expression grew profound and turned inward, and he struck poses which can only be described as meditative. He had acquired, for example, the habit of gazing at the stars. His sensitivity heightened in the same way; I noticed that he was easily brought to tears.

I kept up the lessons with unswerving determination, although without noticeable improvement in outcome. The onerous project had become a tortured obsession, and I reached the point where I felt inclined to use force. My disposition had been slowly warped by my repeated failures, until it turned into a blind animosity towards Yzur. He was becoming moody and withdrawn; in his stubborn silence, he seemed to be brooding, and I began to be convinced that nothing would pull him out of it, when all at once it struck me that he wasn't speaking because he didn't want to.

The cook, horrified, rushed in one evening to announce that he had surprised the monkey "speaking real words". According to the cook, Yzur was squatting next to a fig tree in the garden; but the cook was so shocked he couldn't remember the most essential element - the words. He could only recall two: bed and pipe. I almost kicked him, out of sheer contempt.

Needless to say, I spent the night clutched by great emotion, and that which I had refrained from doing for three long years - the mistake which brought all my efforts to a dead loss - sprang from the restlessness and irritability of that sleepless night, as well as from my own excessive curiosity.

Instead of letting the monkey arrive at the manifestation of language at his own pace, I called to him the following day and ordered him to speak, threatening him with punishment if he didn't obey.

He just jabbered the usual p's and m's of which I'd already had a bellyful, and made with his usual sly, hypocritical winks and, may God forgive me, there was a certain hint of irony in his mocking grimaces.

This infuriated me and, without thinking, I whipped him. This only produced tears and an even deeper silence unbroken even by moans.

Three days later he fell ill, and sank into a sort of dark dementia complicated by symptoms of meningitis. Leeches, cold compresses, purgatives, counterirritants, bromides, alcohol rubs - all possible therapy was brought to bear against the malicious illness. With desperate perseverance, I struggled to carry on, torn by conflicting impulses of remorse and fear. This was because I believed the beast to be a victim of my cruelty; also because I feared for the secret he was perhaps carrying with him to the grave.

After a long, uncertain interval, he began to get better, but he was still so weak that he couldn't get out of bed. The nearness of death had ennobled and humanized him. His eyes, full of gratitude, never took themselves off me, but followed me around the house like two spinning balls, even when I walked behind him. His hand reached out for mine in the intimacy of convalescence. Within the sphere of my self-imposed solitude, he was rapidly acquiring the status of a person.

The demon of scientific inquiry, which is nothing but the embodiment of the spirit of perversity, impelled me, nevertheless, to resume my experiments. In fact the monkey had spoken. But I couldn't simply leave it at that.

I started slowly, asking him the letters he knew how to pronounce. Nothing! I left him alone for hours, spying on him through a peephole in a partition. Nothing! I spoke with him in short sentences, playing on his faithfulness, or his fondness for food. Nothing! When I said something sad, his eyes would brim with tears. When I used a familiar phrase such as "I am your friend", with which I began all our lessons, or with "you are my monkey" with which I always completed my opening statement in order to inspire in him a belief in my total honesty, he signified his agreement by squeezing his eyelids. But he made no sound, nor would he even go so far as to move his lips.

He had resorted to gestures as his sole means of communicating with me and, in view of this newest development, coupled with his other similarities to deaf mutes, I redoubled my precautions, mindful of the predisposition of deaf mutes to mental illness. Sometimes I wished he might go mad, so I could see if delirium would finally loosen his tongue.

During convalescence, his physical condition remain unchanged. The same enfeeblement, the same melancholy. It was clear that this was a sickness of the mind and emotions. His entire organism had been sapped by some sort of brain disorder, and one day soon, I feared, his case would turn hopeless.

Despite the meekness and submissive compliance which his sickness seemed to bring out, his silence, that desperate silence provoked by my demented exasperation, never let up. From some deep well of evolutionary habit, which the eons had petrified into instinct, his race imposed its millennial mutism on the animal, fortifying an atavistic will at the very roots of his being. The primal men of the jungle, subdued and forced into silence - which is to say intellectual suicide - by who knows what barbarous injustice, kept their secret; forest mysteries formed in the abysses of prehistory, and spanning measureless oceans of time, still held in thrall the dark unconscious of this chimpanzee.

The great quadrumane apes of the anthropoid family were left derelict during the march of evolution when humanity took the lead and tyrannized them with barbaric brutality, deposing them and casting them down from the throne from which they had reigned over the arboreal domains of their pristine Eden. Their virid kingdoms ran red with blood when protohuman hunters, intent on their extermination, decimated their numbers ruthlessly, capturing their females, and enslaving both them and their offspring. Vanquished, impotent, the defeated apes asserted what was left of their mortal dignity by severing their one remaining tie with the enemy - the accursed, if superior, tie of speech, and to this desperate act they added the ultimate safeguard of secluding themselves in the supreme night of lower animality.

What horrors, what monstrous atrocities must the conquerors have perpetrated upon these demi-brutes during the ramification of their evolution to prompt them, after they had tasted the enchantments of intellect - which is the paradaisical fruit of the Bible -

to resign themselves to the claudication of their race, and the reduction of their breed to a degraded equality with inferior animals! What inconceivable cruelties must their overlords have inflicted to cause them to consign themselves to a regression which forever crystallized their intellect on a level with the motorized gestures of a wind-up acrobat! What stupendous cowardice of life would eventually stoop their backs in eternal bondage as a mark of their bestial state, and stamp them with the melancholy trepidation and quixotic befuddlement which would become their chief distinguishing features, and render them caricatures of their own nature!

This was why, at the very verge of success, my ill humor was awakened from the bottom of some deep ataviastic limbo. Across millions of years, the word, with its resonant alchemy, went on stirring in the ancient simian soul; but against the temptation which was about to pierce the protective shadows of primordial animal instinct, were set equally powerful ancestral memories, which had instilled in the species an instinctive horror, blocking it like a million-year-old wall.

Yzur commenced his death agony without losing consciousness. He was dying gently, with his eyes closed. His respiration was weak, he had a wandering pulse, and the absolute quiet which surrounded him was interrupted only when, from time to time, he turned towards me, with a heartrending expression of eternity, his face of a sad old mulatto. And the final night, the night of his death, was when the extraordinary thing happened which motivated me to write this account.

Overcome by the warmth and serenity of the twilight, I was dozing at his bedside, when I suddenly felt something seize my wrist.

I awoke with a start. The monkey, with his eyes bulging, was definitely dying this time, and his expression was so human, that it filled me with dismay; but his hand, his eyes, attracted me with such eloquence, that I immediately bent over his face; and then, with his last breath, the last breath that crowned and crushed my hopes at the same time, he uttered - I am sure - uttered in a murmur (how can I describe the tone of a voice that has endured without speaking for ten thousand centuries!) these words whose humanity reconciles our species:

"WATER, MASTER. MASTER, PLEASE. I LOVE...MY MASTER..."

# The Pillar of Salt

Here, according to a pilgrim, is the true history of the monk Pipistratus:

...Anyone who has ever passed by the monastery at Al Saabah says the desolation is indescribable. Imagine an ancient edifice situated on the banks of the Jordan, whose coursing waters are soaked up by the thirsty yellow sands, and drained away until they are almost spent by the time they empty into the bowl of the Dead Sea, among thickets of terebinths and apples of Sodom. As far as the eye can see, there is but a single, solitary stand of palms, whose drooping fronds fringe the walls of the monastery. Over everything hangs an infinite solitude, disturbed each afternoon only by the footsteps of some nomads driving their flocks; a colossal silence amplified by the cusp of mountains whose eminence immures the horizon. When the wind blows in from the desert, it brings an intangible rain of sand; when the wind is from the lake, all the plants are left covered with salt. Dusk and dawn are confounded in the same haze of melancholy. Only those who must expiate terrible crimes grapple with similar solitudes. In the monastery can be heard the sounds of a mass and the taking of communion. The monks, who number no more than five and every one of them at least sexagenarian, offer to wayfarers a modest repast of fried dates, grapes, river water, and sometimes palm wine. They never leave the monastery, although neighboring tribespeople respect them because they are good doctors. When someone dies, they bury him in the caves pocking the riverbanks below the cliffs. Pairs of blue doves, friends of the monastery, now nest in these caves; many years back, they were inhabited by the first hermits, one of whom was the monk Pipistratus whose story I am about to tell. May Our Lady of Carmel help you to listen attentively. That which you are going to hear was recounted to me word for word by Brother Porphyry who now rests in one of the caves at Al Saabah, where he finished his sainted life at eighty years of age in virtue and penitence. May God receive him into His grace. Amen.

Pipistratus was an Armenian monk who had resolved to spend his life in solitude with various young companions drawn from the mundane sphere, and recently converted to the religion of the Crucified One. They belonged to the strenuous sect of the Stylites. After long wanderings in the desert, they found the caves of which I have spoken and installed themselves in them. The waters of the Jordan, the fruits of a small orchard they cultivated in common, were enough to meet their needs. They passed their days praying and meditating. From these grottoes rose columns of prayers, which propped up with their strength the sagging vault of heaven, and kept it from caving in on the sins of this world. For the sacrifice of such exiles, who daily offer up the mortification of their flesh and the pain of their fasts and abstinences to the righteous ire of God, so as to placate Him, avoids many pestilences, wars, and earthquakes. This is something which isn't known by the impious, who smile condescendingly at the penitential practices of cenobites. All the same, the prayers and sacrifices of the just are the keys to the roof of the universe.

At the end of thirty years of austerity and silence, Pipistratus and his companions had attained sainthood. The Demon, conquered, howled with impotence under the feet of the saintly monks. Then they began to end their lives one after another, until Pipistratus was the only one left. He was very old and very thin. He had become almost transparent. He prayed on his knees fifteen hours a day, and had revelations. Every afternoon two friendly doves brought him some pomegranate seeds in their beaks and gave them to him to eat. He lived on nothing else; as a result, he had a pleasant smell like a jasmine bush in the afternoon. Every year, during the dolorous winters, he would wake to find, at the head of his bed of twigs, a gold cup filled with wine and bread and he absorbed this unexpected communion with ineffable ecstasy. It never occurred to him to wonder where this had come from, but then he well knew that the Lord Jesus could have put it there. And he awaited with perfect unction the day of his ascension to the hereafter, as his years continued to mount. Since those years had totaled more than fifty, not a single wayfarer had passed by the lonely monastery.

But one morning, while the monk was praying with his doves, they were suddenly startled, and took flight like pebbles shot from a sling. A pilgrim was standing at the entrance to the cavern. Pipistratus, after greeting him with holy benedictions, pointed to a pitcher of fresh water, and invited him to rest. The stranger drank greedily, as if vitiated by fatigue and, after devouring a fistful of dried fruits which he extracted from his haversack, he joined the monk in prayer.

Seven days elapsed. The wayfarer described his pilgrimmage from Caesarea to the shores of the Dead Sea, concluding his narrative with an account which fascinated Pipistratus.

"I have seen the remains of the cities of sin," he said one evening to his host; "I have seen the sea smoke like a furnace, and I have contemplated, full of fear, the woman of salt, the chastised wife of Lot. The woman is alive, my brother, and I have heard her weep and watched her perspire under the midday sun."

"A similar thing was related by Juvenicus in his treatise *On Sodom*," Pipistratus said in a quiet voice.

"Yes, I know the passage," the pilgrim resumed. "There is something more conclusive in it; and that is that Lot's wife, after her castigation, continued to be physiologically a woman. And I have often thought that it would be an act of charity to liberate her from her condemnation…"

"But, it is God's justice," exclaimed the hermit.

"Didn't Christ also come to redeem with his sacrifice the sins of the ancient world, "the wayfarer suavely rejoined like one learned in sacred literature. "Doesn't baptism cleanse sins against the Law as well as sins against the Evangel?"

After exchanging these words, both dropped off into dreams. It would be the last night they would spend together. The following day the stranger departed, trailed by the blessing of Pipistratus; and it isn't necessary to add, despite his good appearances, that this false pilgrim was Satan in person.

The plan of the Malignant One was subtle. A tenacious obsession assailed the spirit of the saint from that night forward. "Baptize the pillar of salt, and free from her misery this imprisoned spirit!" Charity demanded it, reason argued. In the toils of this struggle months elapsed until in the end, the monk had a vision. An angel appeared to him in his dreams and commanded him to carry out the act.

Pipistratus prayed and fasted for three days and, on the morning of the fourth, setting out from his enclosure of acacias, he took the path paralleling the Jordan, which led down to the Dead Sea. The journey wasn't long, but his feeble legs could barely sustain him. He marched thus for two days. The faithful doves continued to feed him as always, and he prayed constantly, intensely, that God's guiding light might lead him to some resolution of the dilemma so keenly afflicting him. At last, as his legs were about to fail, the mountains opened and the lake appeared.

The skeletons of the dead cities little by little revealed themselves. Some burnt stones and scorched outcroppings were all that remained: rubble from arches, shards of bricks, charred tiles, chunks of masonry rotted by salt and stuck together by tar… The monk tarried as briefly as possible among this wreckage, so as to keep his feet from being contaminated. Suddenly, his old body gave a shudder. He had finally reached the southern shore. He was ankle-deep in dusty debris, at the foot of a forsaken promontory, when he perceived the dim silhouette of a statue.

In its petrified shroud, which centuries of time had gnawed and corroded, it loomed with an ominously imposing stateliness no figment of the imagination could manifest. The sun shone with limpid incandescence, calcinating the boulders, making a mirror of the brackish shawl of salty powder which covered the leaves of the terebinths. These trees, beneath the meridional swelter, appeared to be made of silver. There wasn't a cloud in the sky. The bitter waters slept in their immemorial stillness. When the wind blew, the pilgrims said you could hear the laments of the ghosts of the wicked cities.

Pipistratus approached the statue. The wayfarer had told the truth. A warm moisture covered its face. Its white eyes, its white lips, were completely immobile under the pervasive stone, locked in its dream of the centuries. Not a hint of life emerged from this rock. The sun parched it with its implacable tenacity, always the same for thousands of years; yet this effigy was alive, was a living pillar which perspired! It was as if its dreaming called back the mystery of the biblical terrors. The wrath of Jehovah had passed over this being, this frightful amalgam of flesh and rock. Wasn't he afraid to disrupt this dream? Wouldn't the sin of the accursed woman fall upon any interloper reckless enough to try to rescue her? To awaken mystery is a criminal madness, even a temptation of the inferno. Pipistratus, filled with dismay, knelt down to pray in the shadow of a clump of trees…

How to test the question there was no way to tell. All he knew was that when holy water was sprinkled on the statue, the salt slowly melted away and, in front of the eyes of the hermit a woman appeared, old as eternity, clad in wretched tatters, livid as ash, lank and trembling, dripping centuries. The monk who had seen the Demon without fear, was filled with dread in the face of this apparition. It was the reprobate city and its populace which had risen in her. These eyes had beheld the combustion of the sulfurs, had looked on as the divine fury visited a hail of brimstone on the ignominious cities; those tatters were remnants of the hair and skin of Lot's camels; those feet had trod the ashes of the ovens of eternity! And the frightful woman spoke to him in her ancient voice.

She remembered nothing. Only a vague vision of fire, a tenebrous sensation of waking to the sight of this sea. Her soul was torn by confusion. She had slept too much, her dream was as black as a sepulcher. She suffered without knowing why, submerged in this nightmare. This monk had saved her. She sensed it. It was the only clear thing in her recent vision. And the sea…the fire…the catastrophe…the blasted cities…all this vanished in a clear vision of death. She had been going to die. She would be saved, then. And it was the monk who had saved her!

Pipistratus shivered uncontrollably. A red flame ignited his pupils. His past had been whisked away from him, as if the wind of fire had swept off his soul. One conviction gripped his mind: Lot's wife was there! The sun descended behind the mountaintops. The purples and blood-reds of a mighty conflagration stained the horizon. The tragic days revived in all their awesome, blazing pomp. It was as if a resumption of the punishment were being mirrored a second time by the waters of the bitter lake. Pipistratus had receded down the centuries. He remembered. He had been an actor in the cataclysm. And this woman…this woman had known him…he had known this woman! Then a horrific anxiety seared his flesh. His tongue came untethered and directed itself at the resuscitated specter:

"Woman, tell me what you saw…Speak, I beg you…Can you not reply?"

"Yes," she said, "…You have saved me!"

The anchorite's eyes glistened, as if in them were concentrated all the splendor that lit up the mountains.

"Woman, tell me what you saw when you turned your face to look." In a voice knotted by anguish, she replied:

"Oh, no, by Elohim, you don't want to know. You mustn't ask!"

"Tell me what you saw!"

"No…no…it will mean the abyss!"

"I want to see the abyss."

"It is death…"

"Tell me what you saw!"

"I cannot…I will not!"

"But I have saved you."

"No…no…"

The sun was setting.

"Speak!"

The woman drew closer. Her voice seemed covered with dust, agonized, vanquished, eclipsed. "By your parents ashes," she pleaded.

"Speak!"

Then the specter cupped her hand to the cenobite's ear, and spoke some word. And Pipistratus, fulminated, annihilated, without uttering a cry, fell dead. Pray to God for his soul.

# Psychon

Doctor Paulin, renowned throughout the scientific world as the inventor of the telectroscope, the electrolide, and the negative mirror, of which we will speak more some day, came to this capitol approximately eight years ago, incognito, to avoid crowd scenes, which his modesty repudiated. Our physicians and men of science quickly ferreted out the identity of this august personage, who had tried to maintain anonymity under an assumed name, and which I now make public because of the authority it carries, so that the resolution of any debate which the telling of this story may occasion will not rely, for its sole support, on my proficiency in the scientific arena.

A common case of rheumatism, which rebelled in the face of all treatment, led to my acquaintance with Doctor Paulin when he first settled here in the countryside, still a foreigner. A certain friend, a member of the Society for Psychic Studies, who had recommended the doctor in glowing terms ever since meeting him in Australia, put us in touch. My rheumatism disappeared during heliotherapy treatment pioneered by the doctor; and the gratitude I felt towards him, as well as the interest his experiments held for me, converted our acquaintance into friendship, and developed into sincere affection.

A preliminary glance at the career of this eminent man may serve to assist in the comprehension of what is to follow.

Doctor Paulin was, first and foremost, a distinguished physicist. A disciple of Wroblewski at the University of Cracow, he dedicated himself to the study of the liquefaction of gases, a problem whose germ, planted by Lavoisier, was imaginatively cultivated by Faraday, Cagniard-Latour and Thilorier. But it wasn't only in his unique approach to chemical research that the doctor excelled. He specialized in the more abstruse aspects of the field of suggestive therapeutics, whose terrain had already been trod with valor and distinction by Charcot, Dumontpallier, Landolt, and Luys; and besides engineering the heliotherapeutic method already cited, he was sufficiently revered to be consulted by the likes of such figures as Guimbail and Branly, about topics as recondite and elusive as the conductivity of neurons, the recently established law of which sparked a furor at the time.

I am forced to confess, nevertheless, that Doctor Paulin suffered from a grave defect. He was a spiritualist, having, more's the pity, the frankness to admit it. I always remember, in this connection, the end of a letter which he wrote in July of '98 to Professor Elmer Gates in Washington, replying to another in which were summarized his experiments related to suggestion in dogs and to dirigibility; that is, modifications of behavior elicited by directing the force of the will over specific parts of an organism.

"Well, yes," said the doctor, "You have reasons for your conclusions, which have recently been published together with the story of your experiments in the *New York Medical Times*. The spirit is what governs the organic tissues and the physiological functions, because it is that which creates these tissues and assures their vital faculties. And you know that I feel inclined to diverge from your opinion, etc."

Doctor Paulin was regarded askance by the academics. As with Crookes, as with Rochas, they accepted him only with keen suspicion. He lacked the materialist stamp needed to validate his diploma of knowledge.

Why had Doctor Paulin settled in Buenos Aires? It seems that the cause was a scientific expedition of which the crowning glory was to be the completion of certain botanical investigations related to medicine. Through my mediation, a number of plants were made available for study, including the jarilla, whose emenagogic properties I have described elsewhere, and whose bark is used in making poultices which are said to sharply reduce fever. I asked permission to assist in his experiments, and have been a witness to them ever since.

The doctor had, in Blank Street, a laboratory to which a consulting room was annexed. Those who knew him will remember this and other details, because the man was universally known for his candor and the lack of mystery surrounding his existence. In this laboratory one night, while chatting with the doctor about certain unwritten rites affecting clergymen the world over, he put forward an odd explanation of a centuries-old monastic custom, and I became quite engrossed.

We were discussing tonsures, a practice whose derivation I had been unable to pinpoint, when the doctor suddenly shot me this argument, which I present without amendment:

"I know that you are aware that the fluid emanations of the human body are perceived by sensitives in the form of resplendences: reds, which emerge from the right side, blues, which hover on the left. This law is constant, except in left-handed people, whose polarity switches for the sensitive, in the same way a compass is affected by a magnet. Just before I learned this, I had been experimenting with Antonia, the clairvoyant who was instrumental in testing the electrolide, and found myself in the presence of a fact which made an extraordinary claim on my attention. The sensitive saw, spreading from my occiput, a yellow flame, wavering, and growing ever larger until it reached thirty centimeters in height. The persistence with which the girl affirmed the reality of this occurrence filled me with dread. Though my first impulse was to presume that I was dealing with a case of involuntary suggestion, which was quite prevalent at the time as a result of a method employed by Dr. Luys in this kind of investigation - hypnosis of the retinae only, so as to leave the rational faculties free - I couldn't brush the matter aside."

The doctor rose from his chair, and began to pace up and down the room. "With the fascination which naturally surfaces in reaction to so unexpected a phenomenon," he continued, "I tried an experiment the other day with five boys as paid participants. Antonia could see the mysterious flame in none of them, though she saw some ordinary aureoles; all the more was my surprise to hear her exclaim, in the presence of the porter, Mr. Francis, whom I had summoned as a last resort: This gentleman has one. It's clear, but not as brilliant.' I complained for two days about this phenomenon; until suddenly, because of an old habit of hoarding details acquired in past research, an idea struck me which, at first, seemed slightly ridiculous, but soon won me over."

He puffed vigorously on his cigar, remarking "I have a habit of wearing a cap while I work; baldness obliges me to indulge this impropriety. The day Antonia saw the yellow fulgor above my head, it was while I wasn't wearing my cap, which I had hung on a peg, due to the excessive heat. Could it have been the boys' hair which blocked the emission of flame? According to Fugairon, the fibrous tissue which constitutes the epidermis is a bad conductor of animal electricity; in this sense, hair, and skin tissue as well, possess identical properties. What's more, Mr. Francis is bald like me, and the coincidence of the phenomenon in both of us validates this compelling supposition. My later investigations fully confirmed it; now you will understand the reason the tonsure was instituted as a monastic tradition. Primitive monks observed above the heads of some apostles electrogenes, which is to say, using a term of recent coinage, the resplendence which Antonia perceived in us. This distinctive mark, from Moses forward, is not rare in legendary chronicles. Later, when churchmen began to note the obstacle which hair represents, they established the habit of shaving this point of the skull where the fulgor arises, creating the phenomenon in question, with all the attendant prestige implied, allowing it to be manifested with the fullest intensity. Has my explanation convinced you?"

"It seems to me at least as ingenious as Volney's explanation that the tonsure is the symbol of the sun…"

I was in the habit of contradicting him this way, indirectly, because it spurred him to wrap up his exegeses.

"You must take into account, likewise, the assertions of Brillat-

Savarin, who declared that tonsure was prescribed for monks so that their heads would feel fresh," replied the doctor between annoyance and amusement. "Be this as it may, there's something more," he went on, animatedly. "For some time I had been planning an experiment on these fluid emanations, on the *infralux*, to use the expression of Reichenbach, its discoverer: I wanted to plot the spectrum of these glowing haloes. I tried to re-create, as described by the sensitive, all the minutiae…"

"And the result," I asked enthusiastically.

"The result was a green ray in the indigo band near the red zone, and two blacks in the green band near the blue zone. Bearing in mind also the yellow I discovered, the result is extraordinary. Antonia says she can see in the red a clear violet ray."

"That's absurd!"

"As you wish; but I have formulated a spectrum, and she has indicated to me the position of the ray which she sees or believes she sees. According to these data and allowing a margin for all possible error, I believe that the diffusion number of this ray is 5567. As such, it has a curious identity, since the ray 5567 proves to coincide with the beautiful ray number 4 of the aurora borealis."

"But, Doctor, this is pure fantasy," I exclaimed, alarmed by these vertiginous ideas.

"No, my friend. This simply means that the poles are something like the tops of the skulls of planets!"

Not long after this conversation, whose final phrase was blessed by one of Doctor Paulin's boundlessly affable smiles, he enthusiastically read to me, one afternoon, the first news about the liquefaction of hydrogen effected by Dewar in May of that year, and about the discovery made a few days later by Travers and Ramsay, of three new air elements: krypton, neon, and metargon, precisely outlining the procedure for the liquefaction of gases; and, apropos of these facts, I remember his jeremiad of toil and struggle: "No, no, it isn't possible that I will die without my name being tied to one of these discoveries, which are the glory of a lifetime. Tomorrow morning I will continue my experiments."

The very next day, he set to work, in fact, with febrile ardor;

and though, by this time, I was inured to dread, I couldn't help but shudder when, one afternoon, a very tranquil voice said to me: "Would you believe that I saw with my own eyes a neon ray in the spectrum?

"Really," I asked with undisguised discourtesy.

"Really. I believe this ray has put me on the right path at last. But just to satisfy your curiosity, I feel compelled to address certain questions I had held back from answering before."

I acknowledged him warmly, composed myself, and listened avidly.

The doctor began, "Though information concerning the liquefaction of hydrogen was decidedly limited, my knowledge of the subject permitted me to fill in the blanks, by pressing into service one of Olzewski's apparatuses, used in the preparation of liquid air. Applying afterwards the principle of fractionated distillation, one obtains, like Travers and Ramsay, the spectrum of krypton, neon, and metargon. I arranged to extract these substances later, to see if any new spectral traces appeared in the residue and, in fact, when nothing else was left, the aforementioned ray appeared."

"And how is the extraction effected?"

"The liquid air is slowly evaporated, and the gas released by this evaporation is collected in a receptacle. If you took at this point a Linde machine that subministers seventy kilograms of air per hour, the process could be carried out on a grand scale; but I must content myself with a production of eight hundred cubic centimeters. Trapping the gas in the receptacle, I treat it with heated copper to retain the oxygen, and use a mixture of calcium and magnesium to absorb the nitrogen. That leaves argon isolated; and that is when there appears the double green ray of krypton, discovered by Ramsay. Melting the isolated argon, and subjecting it to slow evaporation, the products of the distillation subministered in the Geissler tube are an orangish-red light, with new rays, which, augmented by the interposition of a Leyden jar, characterize the neon spectrum. If distillation is continued, one obtains a solid product of very slow evaporation, whose spectrum is characterized by two lines, one green and the other yellow, denouncing the existence of metargon or eosium, according to the proposition of Berthelot. Up to now, this was all that was known."

"And the violet ray?"

"We will be seeing it shortly. Consider, meanwhile, how the same result can be achieved by proceeding in another fashion. First, the oxygen and nitrogen are drawn off by means of the indicated substances; later the argon and metargon with hyposulfate of soda; krypton next with phosphorous of zinc, and finally neon with iron cyanide of potassium. This method is empirical. Left exclusively in the collecting tube is a residue similar to hoar-frost, which evaporates with supreme slowness. The resulting gas is my discovery."

I leaned forward so as to better hear these solemn words.

"I studied its physical constants, and was able to determine some of them. Its density is 25, 03, that of oxygen being 16, as is known. I have also determined the longitude of the sound wave in this fluid, and the number encountered permitted me to evaluate the fluctuations in caloric specificity which suggest that it is monoatomic. But the surprising thing is that, in its spectrum, characterized by some violet rays in the red band, the ray 5567 coincides with the number 4 of the aurora borealis, the same as that presented by the yellow fulgor perceived by Antonia above my head."

Before such staggering assertions, I let an innocent question escape. "And what would this substance be, Doctor?"

To my great surprise, he grinned with a satisfied smile.

"This substance,…hmmm! This substance could well be volatized thought."

I sprang from my chair, but the Doctor silenced me with a wave of his hand.

"Why not," he went on. "The brain radiates thought in the form of mechanical force, showing every probability of being able to do the same thing in fluid form. The yellow flame in this case cannot be anything other than the product of cerebral combustion, and the analogy of its spectrum with that of the substance I discovered has made me believe that they are almost identical. Calculate, if you can, the enormous radiation which must be produced by the daily expenditure of thought. What happens to all the useless or strange thoughts, the creations of the imagination, the ecstasies of the mystics, the dreams of hysterics, the projections of illogical minds; what becomes of all those forces whose action is not manifest for lack of immediate application? Astrologers say that thoughts live on the astral plane, likening them to latent forces susceptible to being actuated under certain conditions. Might this not be a premonition of the phenomenon which science is on the road to discovering? As a psychic entity, at least, thought is immaterial; but its manifestations must be fluid, and this is perhaps what I have managed to capture in the laboratory."

Swept away by his theory, the doctor lunged audaciously into one area of inquiry after another, carried along by an awful logic, which I tried in vain to resist.

"I have given my substance the name of *psychon*," he concluded. "You already understand why. Tomorrow we are going to try an experiment: to liquefy thought." (The doctor had conscripted me, as you have seen, as an accomplice in these experiments and, however reluctantly, at times, I found myself hard put to refuse.) "Afterwards, we will calculate whether or not it may be possible to alloy it with some metal, and to store psychic medals. Medals of genius, poetry, audacity, sadness! Later we will determine its location in the atmosphere which, if the expression may be permitted, we shall call the psychosphere, and its corresponding stratum...Until tomorrow at two, then, and we shall see the result of all this".

At two on the dot we were at work.

The doctor pointed out his new apparatus. It consisted of three concentric spirals formed by copper tubes communicating with one another. The gas collected in the outer spiral, under a pressure of six hundred and forty-three atmospheres, and a temperature of -136 degrees, obtained by the evaporation of ethylene according to the circulatory system of Pictet, was funneled back through the other two serpentines, distended into the lower end of the inner spiral and, successively traversing the annular compartments encountered along the way, poured out close to its point of departure at the upper end of the second. The apparatus measured all together 0,70 m of height by 0,175 m of diameter. The distension of the compressed fluid occasioned the decline in temperature required for liquefaction, using the cascade method introduced by Professor Pictet.

Having prudently put in place every safeguard which potential complications demanded, the doctor started his experiment.

Meanwhile, I prepared to record the proceedings as he dictated them to me, in a formulary. For the sake of accuracy, I am reconstructing the events which followed, from my much-redacted notes.

The doctor said, "When the distension reaches four hundred atmospheres, it will obtain a temperature of -237 degrees 3 and the fluid will fill a double-walled flask separated by an empty space of air; the inner wall is plated to impede the transfer of heat by convection or radiation."

"The product is a transparent and colorless liquid that presents certain analogies with alcohol."

"The critical constants of the psychon are four hundred atmospheres and -237 degrees 3."

"A thread of platinum whose resistance is 5038 ohms in melted ice doesn't present resistance of more than 0.119 in the boiling psychon. The law of variable resistance applied to this thread at this temperature fixes the boiling point of the psychon at -265."

"Are you sure this is what you want to say," I asked, brusquely suspending the dictation.

He didn't respond; the situation was too grave.

"What I wish to say," he continued, as if talking to himself, "is that we are only eight degrees from absolute zero."

Anxiously, I began to get up, intending to examine the liquid whose residue clearly adhered to the flask. "Thought!…Absolute zero!…," he stammered, with a certain drunken lucidity, in this world of impossible temperatures.

"If it could be translated," he wondered aloud,"What would be said by this cupful of clear liquid glistening before our eyes? What supreme oration, what child's babble, what criminal intent, what wild schemes, might lie trapped in this receptacle? Or perhaps some disconcerting work of art, some priceless discovery lost in the void of irrationality?"

The doctor, oppressed by an emotion he tried in vain to repress, measured the room with great strides. Finally, he approached the apparatus saying, "The experiment is finished. We must vent the receptacle so that the liquid can escape and evaporate. Let nothing remain lest it cause the oppression of any soul."

He opened a stopcock near the bottom of the flask and, as the liquid began to descend, the dying noise of the escaping substance could be distinctly perceived.

Suddenly, I noted on the face of the doctor a sardonic expression entirely oblivious to everything going on around him; and, almost simultaneously, the outlandishly incongruous idea of jumping onto the nearby table suddenly stole over me and, barely had I begun to think it, when the furniture in question passed under my legs, not without giving me time to see the doctor launching through the air like a ball his beloved cat, a purebread Siamese, which he regarded as his own child. The notebook was on a level with the doctor's snickering nostrils, propelled there by a formidable pirouette made by the doctor in my honor. All I know is that, for more than an hour, we committed the most extravagant escapades, to the complete stupefaction of the neighbors whom the tumult attracted, and to whom we couldn't explain a thing. I remember vaguely that, in the middle of a laugh, ideas of crime assaulted me at the same time as I was buffeted by a vertiginous torrent of mathematical problems. The cat joined in our capers with an ardor foreign to its tropical apathy, and which didn't cease even when the spectators forced open the doors little by little; there could be no doubt that the pure thought we had absorbed was surely the elixir of madness.

Doctor Paulin disappeared the following day, without even taking time to leave a forwarding address.

Yesterday, for the first time, definite news arrived. It seems he repeated his experiment, then was seen in Germany in an asylum.